The MONOCLE
Travel Guide Series

②Ⓜ

New York

For more information,
please visit *gestalten.com*
———
Bibliographic information
published by the Deutsche
Nationalbibliothek: The Deutsche
Nationalbibliothek lists this publication in the Deutsche National-
bibliografie; detailed bibliographic
data are available online
at *dnb.d-nb.de*

This book was printed on
paper certified by the FSC®

Monocle editor in chief:
Tyler Brûlé
Monocle editor: *Andrew Tuck*
Series editor: *Joe Pickard*
Guide editor: *Ed Stocker*
———
Designed by *Monocle*
Proofreading by *Monocle*
Typeset in *Plantin & Helvetica*
———
Printed by *Offsetdruckerei
Grammlich, Pliezhausen*

Made in Germany

Published by *Gestalten*, Berlin 2015
ISBN 978-3-89955-575-2

3rd printing, 2016

Welcome
—— New York
in your pocket

New York has been snapped and filmed a million times: from Alfred Eisenstaedt's famous black-and-white Times Square photo for *Life* magazine in 1945 to the *Bill Cunningham New York* documentary in 2010 and the changing streets of Manhattan in 1961's *West Side Story*. It's depicted as a place of constant hustle and no-nonsense residents; of endless commerce and impossibly tall buildings.

The purpose of this travel guide is to cut through all the imagery and offer you the "local" experience. We don't want to spoon-feed you: we're assuming you know a thing or two about New York's neighbourhoods and that you'll be able to make a decision about battling the hordes at the Empire State Building with or without our advice (OK, so maybe give it a miss). Instead our team of editors and correspondents have applied the same guiding principles of MONOCLE magazine, putting together a list of the *finest places* and experiences the Big Apple has to offer, be it a *luxury hotel* or a cosy unassuming bar for a *late drink*. Where is a good spot for a run? The best place to grab a quiet booth for a *business lunch*? And where to get a fuss-free, *top-notch trim*? And how about all the retail diversity in the city, from luxury brands in *Bergdorf Goodman* to independent design talent in *Dumbo*?

This is New York so options aren't a problem. Read on to explore the city at your own pace and make it a trip to remember. — (M)

Contents
—— Navigating the city

Use the key below to help navigate the guide section by section.

 Hotels

Food and drink

Retail

Things we'd buy

Essays

Culture

Design and architecture

Sport and fitness

Walks

Map
—— The city at a glance

It's easy to forget quite how small Manhattan is until you get here: just 21km long and a handful wide, the advantage is that everything is accessible on foot (unlike the majority of US cities). Indeed, you can easily stroll from the edge of Manhattan in the West Village – facing New Jersey across the Hudson – to the eastern fringes of the island, this time eyeing the borough of Queens from the East River. Street numbers may not be the most adventurous but they're certainly utilitarian; the numbered avenues and letters of Alphabet City, coupled with the grid system, make getting lost quite an achievement.

We've also picked out the key neighbourhoods in Brooklyn and Manhattan on these maps. Beware, though: these boundaries are fluid and often changing. New York's obsession with naming micro neighbourhoods shows no signs of slowing. Happy exploring.

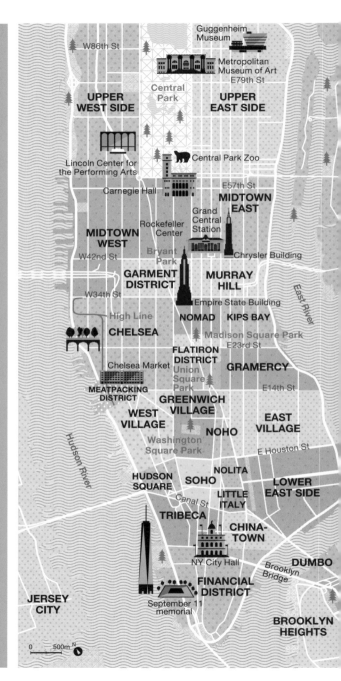

NEW JERSEY

QUEENS

THE BRONX

MANHATTAN

LAGUARDIA
AIRPORT

QUEENS

NEWARK
AIRPORT

BROOKLYN

JFK AIRPORT

GREENPOINT

STATEN
ISLAND

WILLIAMSBURG

Williamsburg
Bridge

MANHATTAN

• Music Hall of Williamsburg

• Continental Army Plaza

BROOKLYN

NAVY YARD

New York
Transit Museum

Forest Park

FORT
GREENE

• Pratt Institute

Brooklyn Academy of Music

DOWNTOWN
BROOKLYN

Atlantic Ave

• Brooklyn Museum

Prospect Park

Need to know
──── Get to grips with the basics

To tip or not to tip? Subway or taxi? And where is the LES compared to Dumbo – and what does LES mean? Read on for some quick facts and helpful information when visiting New York for the first time.

Top tips
Payments

It's never good to make the faux pas of failing to tip adequately in a city where the service industry revolves around client goodwill. As a result of the latter, be prepared for higher percentages than you may have experienced in other corners of the globe. For example, taxi drivers expect 18 to 20 per cent of the bill (if you've had a particularly bad ride you are free to pay less, just make sure your maths is up to scratch). At restaurants and bars you should add about 15 to 20 per cent. That's unless your barman has given your cocktail some serious muddling of course, in which case you might want to be more generous.

Decisions, decisions
Food

The food choice in New York is off the scale which, of course, is a very good thing. However, a word of advice: don't go into a chop-salad bar (or the equivalent) without a reasonably firm notion of what you want. You will find that there is little patience from staff or fellow customers for you to mess around with decision making. As such, our advice is to brush up on the latest food fads in NYC – from açaí berries, flax, maca and quinoa to a well-massaged clump of kale – in order to reap the full culinary and health benefits. Should you be so inclined, there are also plenty of opportunities to try most of the above in liquid form in the city's (somewhat overpriced) juice bars.

Be firm
Etiquette

There's no use being a stuttering, socially awkward individual here: New Yorkers have far too little time for that. This means striking up a conversation with a stranger at a bar or on the subway is often remarkably easy. Good eye contact and a firm shake of the hand are winners – and you can often bypass flowery formalities that go down well in other cultures and be direct. But this doesn't necessarily mean New Yorkers are tactile: go for a North American embrace when meeting someone (that's a hug *sans* kiss) for best results.

Where to be seen
Neighbourhoods

There is a silent war going on in New York and it's over the acceptable places to live in this sprawling metropolis of five boroughs. Fashionistas and creatives simply can't live anywhere above 14th Street: Lower Manhattan and Brooklyn are the only acceptable places. Those on the more traditional (and well-off) Upper East and West Sides might disagree. And those living in Harlem, Astoria and Long Island City might have a thing or two to add to the discussion.

I can give directions as the owl flies

Grass is greener?
Parks

Manhattan's Central Park, opened in 1857, is an obvious centrepiece but you can do better and find less overrun patches along the way. Many New Yorkers choose to look elsewhere for their slice of green space: Prospect Park in Brooklyn is less crowded and has more of a neighbourhood feel, as well as less tension. Its bike loop is popular with cyclists while Prospect Park Lake is a great backdrop for a relaxed Saturday picnic. Fort Greene Park and Pelham Bay Park are also well worth a meander.

Keep it clean
Restaurant ratings

You may notice the A, B or C letter in restaurant windows. Introduced in 2010, these stickers grade the hygiene standards in the city's 24,000-plus restaurants thanks to the city's Department of Health and Mental Hygiene, which shows up unannounced at various venues to check that there are no rats scurrying around the kitchen. While we recommend you stick to the As, judge by the crowds when mulling over entering a B establishment. And it's pretty safe to say that a C rating is a no-no.

Express delivery
Trains

Different trains running on the same platforms on the New York subway can get a little confusing for new arrivals. Local (a train that stops at every station) versus express (stopping at only the key ones) is the main conundrum. Make sure you double check before hopping aboard, otherwise you might find you've shot up most of the length of Central Park unintentionally. Another word of warning: express trains run as local trains late at night but "late" isn't always that clear. So imagine it's 23.30: an A (express) train may be showing that it is an A but is in fact running as a local C train. Confused? Just ask a fellow passenger before jumping aboard.

At a crossroads
Taxis

There is absolutely no use getting into a yellow cab and giving the driver a street address, complete with number: he or she will probably have no idea where it is. New York is built on a grid system so you have to give the cross-street and the biggest nearby intersection. Of course, you could always order a rival cab service on your phone and then it is just a case of keying in the destination address.

High spirits
Alcohol

Learn how to keep it local *like* a local. There is a wealth of New York City (and state) produce to be tried, none better than some fine local tipples that mostly come out of Brooklyn. The eponymous beer brewery is the most obvious but go for something less known. Widow Jane bourbon perhaps; we are big fans of the brand's Cacao Prieto head-quarters in Red Hook (*see page*

I'd rather be drinking bourbon

116). Or, further afield, you can try a chardonnay from Long Island or the Finger Lakes to the north.

Initial thoughts
Acronyms

Right, so you may know your JFK from your NYPD but there's so much more. First up, we'll ease you in with the neighbourhoods: Soho (South of Houston Street), Dumbo (Down Under The Manhattan Bridge), Tribeca (Triangle Below Canal Street), UES/LES (Upper/Lower East Side), UWS/LWS (Upper/Lower West Side) and Fidi (Financial District). Then there's transport: Path (Port Authority Trans-Hudson), BQE (Brooklyn-Queens Expressway), MTA (Metropolitan Transport Authority)… we could go on.

*Is it a bird?
Is it a plane?
Is it Dumbo?*

Hotels
—— At home in the Big Apple

Let's face it, arriving at your hotel room in New York (and Manhattan in particular) can be a bit of a shock to the system. "You can't be serious," is a common refrain, upon entering what turns out to be your tiny home for the next few days. Population density and sky-high property prices can have that effect on a city's hotels and New York is a prime example.

Just bear in mind two key things and you'll be onto a winner: firstly, book well in advance (rooms get snapped up) and make sure you know what you're after. Broadly speaking there are two categories of hotels: the industrial, slightly sparse look that goes with the area (LES or Brooklyn) and the more traditional places (the West Village or UES perhaps). Hotel bars and restaurants are destination venues in this city whether you're a guest or not (which can be a bonus) but make sure you check the late-night and weekend scene if partying isn't your thing.

①
Four Seasons, Midtown
Inspirational interiors

We'd be remiss if we didn't throw in a few standouts in the world of big-chain hotels. That's why the recently refreshed Four Seasons Hotel made our list. The well-known global brand updated the 52-storey property in 2015, including the public areas and all 368 rooms. Renowned Chinese-born American architect IM Pei was the man behind the original design.

The public spaces of the hotel boast 10-metre-high ceilings and are finished with limestone; many of the rooms have unbeatable views of Central Park. For all its grandeur, this property is still nestled in what can be an impossibly noisy and overrun part of New York. Still, the hotel manages to be something of a hideaway. If you're partial to high-end shopping and the ever-present hum of Manhattan, a stay here might well be a win.

What's more, the hotel is just steps away from theatres and the Midtown business district. If you don't plan on staying here you should at least stop by to catch a glimpse of the interiors.
57 East 57th Street, NY 10022
+1 212 758 5700
fourseasons.com/newyork

MONOCLE COMMENT: The 52nd-floor penthouse offers one of the best views of New York's skyscraper skyline that you're likely to find. This is a place where you truly feel like you're in the thick of it.

②
The Park Hyatt New York, Midtown
Lap of luxury

This was built to be the global flagship for the world-renowned brand and it is obvious that the chain was not in a frugal mood. The major factor setting the hotel apart from others is the room size. Located in a Midtown skyscraper, Park Hyatt's 210 rooms are some of the most spacious in Manhattan (there is also a collection of art installations spread throughout the property).

Canadian interior-design firm Yabu Pushelberg says that it was important to create a modern yet residential feel to the hotel, something that would turn Park Hyatt into a meeting point for visitors and New Yorkers alike. Something not to be missed is the elegant ballroom which forms a perfect cube with illuminated white onyx walls.

For some sanctuary head to the 25th-floor spa where you can lie in a pool equipped with underwater speakers (playing specially commissioned music from Carnegie Hall, naturally) and get an impressive view of Central Park.
153 West 57th Street, NY 10019
+1 646 774 1234
newyork.park.hyatt.com

MONOCLE COMMENT: For one of the hospitality industry's most reliable brands this is a suitably indulgent flagship; French architect Christian de Portzamparc has done a fine job. Plus there's the bonus of being right next to Carnegie Hall.

③ The Crosby Street Hotel, Soho
Niche appeal

Soho is not known for its wide pavements, leaving little room to breathe when the masses descend on the world-famous district. Near the hustle – but just far enough from the bustle – is the Crosby Street Hotel. It is set back off the street, making it feel a little bit like the larger, grander hotels uptown.

But that's where comparisons end. Each of the hotel's 97 rooms has its own unique décor. Mannequins in every room are clear nods to the surrounding fashion businesses and various nice touches tie to some of the Crosby's sister hotels in London. Designer and co-owner Kit Kemp knew these details would help set the properties apart.

Once you check in, enjoy the Crosby Bar's afternoon-tea service in the leafy courtyard. Or take some time to notice the canine theme that runs throughout the property, especially the painted mug of a mongrel hung to greet guests at reception. But don't be fooled; this place hasn't gone to the dogs. Management assures us the doggy art merely reflects the abundance of four-legged friends that locals keep as pets.
79 Crosby Street, NY 10012
+1 212 226 6400
firmdalehotels.com

MONOCLE COMMENT: The hotel works well for business travel and fun weekends. The rooms are the thing: pull back the curtains and gaze across the water-butt-adorned rooftops of Soho.

④
Ace Hotel, Nomad
Creative spirit

The dimly lit Ace Hotel exudes an essence of cool. Its constantly bustling lobby welcomes guests and passers-by who lounge on dark leather sofas to drink coffee from Portland coffee roaster Stumptown by day and cocktails by night.

The hotel's rooms evoke the feeling of being in a New York apartment overlooking the brick surroundings of Manhattan's Nomad district. "We keep the geographical touches prevalent," says one staffer. In that vein The Breslin restaurant provides round-the-clock room service in true New York fashion.

Though it has a youthful sensibility, the standards of the Ace remain top notch. No detail is overlooked, from the custom Wings + Horns robes to the unique tapestry artwork and the record players in the rooms.
20 West 29th Street, NY 10001
+1 212 679 2222
acehotel.com

MONOCLE COMMENT: If you want a party hotel this is the one for you: there always seems to be a throng of creatives imbibing cocktails in the lobby and a DJ at the decks. If it gets too much you can retire to the oyster bar next door.

Suite dreams
—
Rooms feature a raft of design-led products

Hotel art

01 **The Quin Hotel, Midtown:** A revolving exhibition in the lobby has featured many big names in the contemporary-art world, including street-art pioneer Blek le Rat and Irish painter Patrick Graham.
thequinhotel.com

02 **The Lexington, Midtown East:** There are works shown around the bars of the Lexington, plucked from hothouses of new talent such as Arthouse at Brooklyn Flea and the Creative Growth Art Center in California. Of note are the jazz portraits by Alex Asher Daniel.
lexingtonhotelnyc.com

03 **The Carlyle, Upper East Side:** Look out for the Arcadian murals in the Carlyle Café by the Hungarian Marcel Vertès and those in the Bemelmans Bar, daintily decorated by the famed author of the *Madeline* picture books, Ludwig Bemelmans.
rosewoodhotels.com

04 **Wythe Hotel, Williamsburg:** If you can, reserve one of the west-facing rooms on the first few floors that look onto a wall of old-school graffiti by New York's Stephen Powers, commissioned specifically for the Wythe.
wythehotel.com

05 **The James Hotel, Lower Manhattan:** Each of the 14 guest floors shows the work of a different artist. If you're passing through, don't miss the mural in the foyer by St Louis artist Sarah Frost, fashioned from pieces of old keyboards.
jameshotels.com

⑤ The Greenwich Hotel, Tribeca
Home comforts

Tribeca's Greenwich Hotel is designed to offer guests every comfort expected from a luxury stay while making you feel right at home. You get the impression that you're staying in someone's guest room thanks to spaces that are all different, with changing textiles and marble work in the bathrooms. From the Japanese-inspired Shibui spa (open daily from 09.00 to 21.00) and private yoga sessions to the guest-only drawing room and courtyard, staying at the warmly lit, rustic-style hotel will make you forget you are still on the bustling island of Manhattan.

If searching for a premium stay, opt for the penthouse. The rooftop sanctuary, designed in the Japanese spirit of *wabi-sabi*, has three bedrooms as well as a huge expanse of outdoor space. And if you want to mix things up a little? There's a restaurant of urban Italian cooking by Andrew Carmellini.
377 Greenwich Street, NY 10013
+1 212 941 8900
thegreenwichhotel.com

MONOCLE COMMENT: The Shibui spa here could easily fit into the design section of this guide; the owners brought in a team of carpenters from Japan to build the space. And it offers far more than just massage: think a pool, fitness room and lounge.

Rock steady

Among the green outdoor space belonging to the penthouse are a series of beautiful stones (used in the benches and plunge pool). It wasn't easy getting them there: sourced from the Hudson Valley, they were hoiked onto the top floor thanks to a crane.

⑥
The Mark, Upper East Side
Avant garde accents

The building housing the elegant
Mark hotel has been sitting on
the corner of 77th Street and
Madison Avenue since 1927. After
undergoing a facelift courtesy of
French interior designer Jacques
Grange in 2009, the demure and
subdued building was transformed
into a 100-room and 50-suite
hotel with chic but avant-garde
design. Red accents offset a striking
op-art marble floor in the lobby – a
theme you'll find even on its fleet
of bicycles and dog bowls (if you
choose to bring a furry friend).

While The Mark is within
walking distance of some of
Manhattan's most exclusive shops,
you can also revel in the pleasure
of having in-house services such
as a John Lobb shoe-shine kiosk
and delicatessen from the Parisian
patisserie Ladurée. Also be sure to
check out the acclaimed restaurant
that is headed by top chef Jean-
Georges Vongerichten.
25 East 77th Street , NY 10075
+1 212 744 4300
themarkhotel.com

MONOCLE COMMENT: We love the
striking monochrome as you walk
into the lobby here. There are
some decadent touches, sure,
but it's very New York.

*If this
breaks it's
Ladurée's
fault*

Make a Mark
———

If the thought of leaving The Mark after a stay gets a bit much you can always, well, stay. The hotel has several three to five-bedroom residences ("Penthouses Extraordinaires") should you wish to come home to a hotel every night. The location isn't too shabby either.

7

The Marlton Hotel,
Greenwich Village
Parisian charm

It's not hard to see why you might
want to spend an afternoon curled
up on a sofa in the lobby here.
The low ceilings and warm wood
finishes are part upstate New York
hunting club and part Paris's 4th
arrondissement. Floor-to-ceiling
windows lined with sheer curtains
allow for surprisingly hidden views
of the street and let lobby-lounging
voyeurs enjoy the mix of passers-by
while swilling a smooth whisky.

The French undertones at this
Greenwich Village property are
deliberate. The owners say they
took inspiration from the grand
hotels of Paris when fitting out the
former New School dormitory. The
rooms are tight but well appointed
and the local products on offer in
the mini bar will charm the pants
off you (or anyone else with whom
you'd care to share a chamber). At
the back of the hotel is a cocktail
bar lined with cherry-red stools
and booths for a midday or late-
night libation. For breakfast and
dinner the dining room, Margaux,
is a twist on French bistros without
a stuffy maître d'. The Marlton
doesn't take itself too seriously.
5 West 8th Street, NY 10011
+1 212 321 0100
marltonhotel.com

MONOCLE COMMENT: Mixing modern
and classic can go disastrously
wrong; we've seen it happen many
a time with hotel design. But the
Marlton pulls it off: historic, yes –
Jack Kerouac wrote two novels here
– but undeniably comfortable.

*This stay
might
inspire my
first Beak
Generation
novel*

(8)
The Nomad, Nomad
Boutique with buzz

The lovingly restored turn-of-the-century building that houses Nomad sits in the heart of the newly branded district of the same name, just north of Madison Square Park. Designed by Jacques Garcia, the interior is richly detailed using handmade textiles, Persian rugs, bespoke furniture and artwork in every room. The overall feeling is romantic, warm and seductive.

Like its sister property the Ace Hotel (*see page 18*), collaboration has been a large part of The Nomad's success. Paris-based brand Maison Kitsuné has its only US store on the ground floor while the charming library has been stocked by Thatcher Wine, owner of Colorado publisher Juniper Books.

But perhaps the star of the show is The Nomad's restaurant, run by Daniel Humm and Will Guidara of Eleven Madison Park. Visitors can dine in a variety of spaces, from the stately Parlour to the bright and airy Atrium. Each dish is a harmonious marriage of a few cleverly chosen flavours, refined without being fussy. It's a reflection of The Nomad as a whole, which strikes a note between sophistication and informality.
1170 Broadway, NY 10001
+1 212 796 1500
thenomadhotel.com

MONOCLE COMMENT: Hotels can often shirk on desks when decking out rooms. But among the many attributes at The Nomad, the mahogany writing tables in rooms are something to admire.

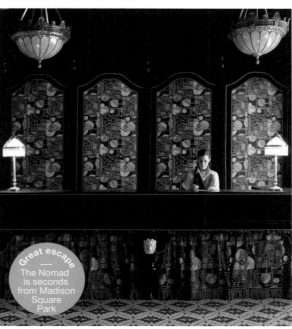

Great escape
—
The Nomad is seconds from Madison Square Park

I plan to beat jetlag from a mid-century armchair

⑨

The High Line Hotel, Chelsea
Understated chic

The brick façade of the High Line Hotel might fool the unsuspecting passer-by. A former seminary, the building comes by its modest appearance honestly. The hotel is a slice of old-school New York in a neighbourhood that is increasingly modernising.

The front courtyard is dotted with bistro tables and a row of planters; a great spot to sit and have a cappuccino from the vintage Intelligentsia coffee truck at the far end of the space. In the summer the patio sheds its daytime caffeine crowd and becomes Champagne Charlie's, where guests and locals gather.

The property has become a de facto retreat from the glam-heavy establishments in the nearby Meatpacking District. The hotel's 60 rooms are understated yet well kept and offer a smart mix of accents from classic to mid-century. This place reminds you that a stay in New York doesn't have to be all pomp; it just has to be about pride of ownership.
180 10th Avenue, NY 10011
+1 212 929 3888
thehighlinehotel.com

MONOCLE COMMENT:
Architecturally this is one of New York's most unusual hotels. Be sure to check out the Harry Potter-esque Hoffman Hall, a high-ceilinged, turn-of-the-century conference space that is a fine example of collegiate gothic architecture.

The Ludlow Hotel, Lower East Side
Diamond in the rough

Though the youngest hotel on our list, The Ludlow bears comparison with some of the top in New York's hospitality scene. As little brother to properties such as The Bowery and The Marlton, its pedigree ensures guests are in good hands. Discreetly situated in the narrow Lower East Side, The Ludlow's stylishly dark entrance and lobby bar are an upscale tip of the hat to the once gritty rock'n'roll neighbourhood. Public space, which includes the 1980s-inspired Dirty French restaurant, is confined to the first floor, giving guests complete privacy upstairs. There, 187 guest rooms offer a calming oasis without losing their cool Lower East Side vibe.

Much like its compact surroundings, rooms are petite – barring custom Indo-Peruvian four-poster beds as the centrepiece. With plenty of mid-rise buildings around, opting for a room above the seventh floor, complete with a glass-fronted sitting room, means unadulterated city views. It's perfect for overlooking busy downtown while relaxing in one of the custom Martin Margiela robes.
180 Ludlow Street, NY 10002
+1 212 432 1818
ludlowhotel.com

MONOCLE COMMENT: A hotel true to its roots in the former tenement district of New York. The Ludlow retains the industrial look of the building it is housed in – and with it some of the history of the neighbourhood.

Soho Grand Hotel, Soho
A place to peacock

This part of Soho was a very different place back in 1996 when the Grand opened: industrial and a little grubby, a far cry from the shopping mecca that it is today. But the gamble has clearly paid off.

The hotel – 353 rooms set over 17 floors – has tried to maintain some of the Soho rough-around-the-edges vibe of yesteryear with an iron-clad staircase designed by Studio Sofield that takes you up to the reception. Sofield is also behind the vast metal birdcages – home to sculptural white peacocks – that dominate the Grand Bar. Peacocks are not the only animals on display: look out for dog statues, a nod to the pet-friendly policy on certain floors. And if you're separated from your fluffy friend during a business trip? The hotel has goldfish – bizarrely – that it can lend out to keep you company.

Rooms come with mini bars stocked with local produce and bedside tables all have Tivoli radios. Be sure to ask for a suite facing north for a skyline view; west if you want to see the sun set over the Hudson.
310 West Broadway, NY 10013
+1 212 965 3000
sohogrand.com

MONOCLE COMMENT: If being downtown is your thing then this hotel is in the perfect location. Rooms can be New York small but it works and there's also a good staff vibe.

Holy roller
The hotel was newly constructed when it opened in 1996; the site previously housed a church. The carpet in the Soho Grand bar is inspired by the old building and one of the original walls forms the edge of the hotel's dog park.

1 Ⓗ **New York**
Hotels ───────

⑫

Wythe Hotel, Williamsburg
Local influence

Wythe Hotel stands perched on
the edge of Brooklyn overlooking
the East River and Manhattan.
Housed in a former textile
factory built in 1901, the venture
from New York restaurateur
Andrew Tarlow feels like a local
affair. There are neighbourhood
touches everywhere, from the
farm-fresh ingredients cooked
over a wood fire at The Reynard
to the hotel's custom furniture
and wallpaper courtesy of
Brooklyn-based company
Flavor Paper.

The majority of Wythe's
sizeable rooms feature large
floor-to-ceiling windows to take
in unobstructed views of the
water and are furnished with
custom-made beds that use
reclaimed ceiling pine by local
woodworker DHWWD. For a bit
of socialising without losing sight
of the picturesque view head to
the white-hot Ides Bar where
you can take in Manhattan's
sparkling skyline while enjoying
a carefully prepared cocktail.
80 Wythe Avenue, NY 11249
+1 718 460 8000
wythehotel.com

MONOCLE COMMENT: The
Williamsburg neighbourhood
has change dramatically in
recent years. However this is
an establishment that not only
remains the same but also
continues to set the standard.
Worth a visit for the rooftop
bar alone.

*Barkeep,
I think
I've found
my perfect
perch*

Family affair

Marlow Goods, a shop inside Wythe Hotel, is run by Kate Huling, the wife of founder Andrew Tarlow. The shop stocks everything from Icelandic wool rugs to leather goods and unisex worker jackets.

⑬
Sixty Soho, Soho
It all adds up

Opened under a new name in early 2015, Sixty Soho is the hotly anticipated work of British interior-design studio Tara Bernerd & Partners and hotelier Jason Pomeranc. Expect glass, steel and velvety flourishes, plus rooms with pictures commissioned by British artist Harland Miller. At the Gordon Bar an eclectic collection of flowerpots and old maps blends with bouncy sofas; for food there's New York restaurateur John McDonald's menu at Italian-themed Sessanta to peruse. Then there's Above Sixty Soho: a roof terrace sure to top the city's socialite's tick-list.
60 Thompson Street, NY 10012
+1 212 431 0400
sixtyhotels.com

MONOCLE COMMENT: Tara Bernerd & Partners is also responsible for the interiors of the Thompson Chicago, Swissotel Zürich and the UK's Center Parcs Treehouses.

Hotel take-homes

01 **Bo the Bear, Bowery Hotel:** A night spent at The Bowery Hotel comes with a cuddly chap in your bed. The dapper teddy – dressed as a bellhop in a little red jacket sporting the hotel's logo, as well as black shorts and a black hat – is perfect for a take-home reminder of your stay.
theboweryhotel.com

02 **Linens by Sferra, The Standard East Village:** Sferra has been the maker of luxury Italian-made linens since 1891 and an in-room line can be purchased. A prime choice to make home feel like a holiday.
standardhotels.com

03 **Denim robe, Hôtel Americano:** It's the best of Americana made for lounging. This Mexican-made cotton denim robe (who knew that could work?) was made exclusively for Hôtel Americano – you've got to see it to believe it.
hotel-americano.com

04 **Pendleton × Ace blanket, Ace Hotel:** With plaid designed by Pendleton, this slate number is made with non-scratchy wool and comes embossed with a label of gratitude: "Thanks for sleeping with us".
acehotel.com

05 **Cade 26 Le Labo Candle, The Gramercy Hotel:** This smoky scented candle – with wood and leather notes – is a signature touch at The Gramercy Hotel. It's made of sox wax and has a cotton wick.
gramercyparkhotel.com

Food and drink
—— Diners' club

It may have something to do with the tip culture but service in New York is slick. Waiters here know they have to work for that 20 per cent; whatever the reasons, you'll be well attended (a little too well on occasion).

The restaurant scene is diverse and international, claiming to be the best in the US (Los Angelenos and Chicagoans would disagree). As you'd expect in a city as diverse as this one, you can get whatever you want whenever you want it. Indeed, unlike Paris or London, which can feel a little conservative, establishments here are relaxed about what time you eat. And whether you're propping up the bar or at a corner table, drinks are just as important; your mind may boggle at the cocktail list (often requiring a glossary).

Whether you're in a small West Village bar or Soho restaurant, what's undeniable is the enthusiasm for going out: New Yorkers socialise outside their homes so you'll always dine with the people who live here.

Restaurants
Pick of the top tables

Legume boom
—
Look out for seasonal veg specialities

 The Fat Radish, Lower East Side
Vegetarian comfort food

The name sounds like a British gastropub and the distressed decor and bench seating wouldn't look out of place in a corner of Marylebone. But while the owners may be British, there's a very New York feel to this intimate Lower East Side diner.

The food, true to its name, is heavily vegetable based (a glimmering plate of peppery radishes awaits diners) with organic offerings sourced from nearby small-scale suppliers. "We're totally driven by seasonal vegetables at the centre of every dish," says Ben Towill, co-founder with Phil Winser (*pictured*). "It's lighter everyday food." The menu constantly changes according to what's in season but save room for the seared tuna with watermelon and jalapeño.
17 Orchard Street, NY 10002
+1 212 300 4053
thefatradishnyc.com

②
Sushi Nakazawa, West Village
Japanese fine dining

Daisuke Nakazawa has travelled
a long way since he started as
an apprentice under celebrated
sushi chef Jiro Ono in 2001. He
was subsequently spotted by
restaurateur Alex Borgognone who
insisted he open his own place.

Housed in a former hair salon,
the tiny space has a 10-seat bar
area (alongside regular tables)
where diners can get close to
Nakazawa as he meticulously
prepares the 20-course *omakase*
menu with local scallops and tuna
flown in from Japan. The interior is
sparse yet warm. Book in advance.
23 Commerce Street, NY 10014
+1 212 924 2212
sushinakazawa.com

③
Russ & Daughters,
Lower East Side
Homely Jewish fare

This veteran Jewish deli was opened
by Joel Russ on East Houston
back in 1914 and it has changed
little since then, a time-warp
establishment serving fish-based
takeaway fare and now run by the
fourth-generation Russ family.

"Food is a conduit for memory
and most of our important
memories revolve around family,"
says Niki Russ Federman (*pictured*),
co-owner and great-granddaughter
of Joel. Recommended nibbles
are the signature pastrami-cured
smoked salmon (on a bagel,
obviously) and the "heebster"
(whitefish and baked salmon salad
with horseradish dill cream cheese).

The latest offshoot, which
opened in 2014, is a sit-down café
located just around the corner on
Orchard Street. Secure yourself
a lunchtime pew at the bar and
order from one of five types of
caviar and blini, washed down with
a crisp glass of white. The pickled
herring trio – canapés in three
varieties on pumpernickel bread –
is also excellent.
179 East Houston Street, NY 10002
+1 212 475 4880;
127 Orchard Street, NY 10002
+1 212 475 4881
russanddaughters.com

It's always
best to
start with
a light
appetiser

As seen on TV
—
Daisuke Nakazawa was
spotted by Alex Borgognone
when he appeared in *Jiro
Dreams of Sushi*, a 2011
documentary about his
master Jiro Ono. The film
charts the work and family life
of the man lauded as one of
the world's greatest
sushi chefs.

④
ABC Cocina, Flatiron District
Mexican reimagination

The same chic and calming glow
that permeates ABC Carpet &
Home continues in the adjacent
dining room at ABC Cocina. The
team led by Michelin-star chef
Jean-Georges Vongerichten serves
up a mix of small and large plates
of refined and reinterpreted
Mexican cuisine, all leaning
towards food that is seasonal
and wholesome.

Expect to find a full range of
options for both vegetarians and
carnivores; think sweet potato
and smoked cherry-pepper
empanadas, lime and mole-
mushroom tacos with sautéed
kale or mescal-cured salmon with
a cucumber-yoghurt relish. We
strongly recommend reserving a
table with friends and planning to
indulge in a mix of shared plates;
there isn't a wrong choice to be
found on the menu.
38 East 19th Street, NY 10003
+1 212 677 2233
abchome.com

⑤
Café Gitane, Nolita
Maghreb-style pit stop

This petite French-Moroccan
operation is well worth the wait
(it can be hard to find a table
during dinner rush hour). Whether
it's the colourful striped umbrellas,
simple café-style tables or retro
mustard-coloured cash register, this
small Nolita restaurant delights.
Dishes are prepared behind the
tiny counter by staff in cobalt-
blue jumpsuits. Enjoy grilled
aubergine with tapenade, goat's
cheese and pesto over watercress
or couscous, while sipping on a
light lillet blanc. This charmer is
perfect for scene-watching.
242 Mott Street, NY 10012
+1 212 334 9552
cafegitanenyc.com

⑥
Glasserie, Greenpoint
Fusion power

Set in a former 1860s glass-fixture
factory on the northern edge
of Brooklyn, this Greenpoint
destination is worth the trek even if
your main digs are in Manhattan.
Owner Sara Conklin and her team
regularly make small changes to the
menu, which is determined by the
produce available at nearby farms.

"Our food philosophy is to
respect the original product by
limiting how much we manipulate
it," says Conklin. Expect colourful,
meticulously presented dishes that
can include house-cured sardines
or rabbit loin.
95 Commercial Street, NY 11222
+1 718 389 0640
glasserienyc.com

Below stairs
—
Private dining is in the moodily lit vault

⑦
Bacaro, Lower East Side
Rough-edged elegance

Leave behind the area's busy streets and find a quiet corner in this Venetian restaurant where wooden tables are lit by blown-glass chandeliers. Founded in 2007 by Kama Geary and Frank DeCarlo, the chef at Nolita's Peasant (*see page 40*), the Italian gastropub features a marble-top bar and private dining in the vaulted catacombs below. Start with a glass of Veneto red and *cichetti* snacks, then *polpette* (spicy meatballs) followed by spaghetti *nero* (pasta with cuttlefish ink). The homemade tiramisu rounds things off.
136 Division Street, NY 10002
+1 212 941 5060
bacaronyc.com

Where you'll find our editors in Soho

Gasoline Alley Coffee: For a flat white to take away.
Crosby Street Hotel: Afternoon tea.
Kelley and Ping: For a casual Asian lunch.
Dominique Ansel Bakery: For the sweetest of treats.
Estela: Dinner.

New York pizza

No trip would be complete without at least a slice of the city's thin-crust offering.

01 **Roberta's, Williamsburg:** Situated among the converted warehouses of Bushwick in Brooklyn, Roberta's draws a fashionable crowd from the area. No reservations are taken for parties smaller than 10 and weekend wait times can be a couple of hours, so grab a drink among the picnic tables at the *tiki*-style outdoor bar. The "Bee Sting" pizza with chilli flakes and honey is a must due to its irresistible sweet-and-spicy combination.
robertaspizza.com

02 **Marta Pizza, Nomad:** Make room for this establishment's wood-oven-cooked, fine-crusted fare; the carbonara pizza is recommended.
martamanhattan.com

03 **Joe's Pizza, Flatiron District:** Joe's has been selling timeless, no-frills New York pizza day and night since 1975 and is known for its signature Sicilian square slice.
joespizzanyc.com

It takes days to get the mozzarella out of my feathers

True south
—
Try some
lesser-known
Mexican
dishes

(8)
Tacombi, Nolita
Camping out

Kitsch and colourful, this Mexican taco joint does a roaring lunchtime trade. An open-plan eating area is dominated by metal camping-style tables and chairs and a parked-up orange Volkswagen camper van that has had its top removed. But the menu is refreshingly simple, with classics such as barbacoa and pork-belly tacos alongside a selection of lesser-known offerings such as Veracruzana fish, all accompanied by an array of spicy sauces. Also worth a punt is the whitefish ceviche starter and the selection of freshly squeezed juices.
267 Elizabeth Street, NY 10012
+1 917 727 0179
tacombi.com

(9)
Blue Hill, Greenwich Village
Village fare

Hidden a few steps below ground level in Greenwich Village, Blue Hill is restrained and discreet. The restaurant lets the food speak for itself: ingredients are sourced from nearby farms – including Blue Hill's own – and the menu shifts with harvests. The dining room can seat up to 50 customers and a celery-root risotto and Berkshire pork with squash bolognese are among chef Dan Barber's creations. Book in advance for the six-course tasting menu, enticingly known as the "Farmer's Feast".
75 Washington Place, NY 10011
+1 212 539 1776
bluehillfarm.com

(10)
Socarrat, Nolita
Paella principal

The Spanish have a name for the crunchy and salty lining that forms on the bottom of a paella pan. A nice layer of *socarrat* is a sign that those in the kitchen know what they are doing so it's only fitting that this paella bar takes its name from the staple of rice, spice and (usually) seafood. This place is not for light eaters. Portions are generous and paella is priced for a minimum of two people. More traditional versions of the dish are on offer but we'd suggest you spice things up with the *fidueà de pato*: paella made with duck confit.
284 Mulberry Street, NY 10012
+1 212 219 0101
socarratrestaurants.com

Must-try

Lobster roll from Greenpoint Fish & Lobster Co, Greenpoint

It's no wonder the lobster roll here tastes so fresh: co-owner Vinny Milburn rises every morning at 04.30 to buy his day's selection from local sellers. "My standards are impossibly high," he says.

Milburn and partner Adam Geringer-Dunn sell out of about 90kg of lobster every day at this fishmonger and restaurant. The shellfish is seasoned with tarragon, lemon and a touch of mayo, then served on a gently grilled bun. It steals the show but a fine selection of raw items are also on offer, such as live sea scallops with seared roe. This tiny space is a real neighbourhood find; be prepared to wait as bar seating is limited.

greenpointfish.com

(11)

Red Farm, West Village
Dim-sum delights

Sometimes you want good Chinese food without having to immerse yourself in the bustle of Chinatown. It can be hard to bag a table here but the end result is worth it. The dim-sum menu is not to be missed, nor the pan-fried pork buns.

If you feel like sharing, dishes such as mussels and clams with green curry or seared bean curd with grooved summer squash are just the ticket. The locale is a short walk from the Monocle Shop – it may just prove the perfect pairing of lunch and retail therapy.

529 Hudson Street, NY 10024
+1 212 792 9700
redfarmnyc.com

Hooked on a feeling
——
Lobster is a billion-dollar industry in the US; the majority of it fished from the northeast coast (Maine, New York and Massachusetts). Alongside the ever-popular lobster roll we're also big fans of the ultimate comfort food: lobster mac'n'cheese.

Must-try

New Zealand red deer with flavours of gin from The Musket Room, Nolita

This simply decorated Michelin-starred restaurant serves modern Kiwi cuisine with Asian influences and is big on game and unusual fruits, vegetables and berries. Tender deer is served in perfectly sized portions: succulent pink meat with a liquorice-and-juniper mousse, caramelised fennel and celeriac purée that combine to imitate the titular "flavours of gin" without actually using the spirit at all.
musketroom.com

12
Veselka, East Village
Late-night stalwart

Maybe it's the eclectic crowd that fills this place at 03.00 after a big night out. Or maybe it's the perfection with which the cooks pore over the preparation of *pierogi*, cabbage rolls and cheese *blintzes*. Whatever it is, it has kept Veselka in business since 1954. The Ukrainian soda shop-cum-greasy spoon is an all-hours holdout in a neighbourhood that has seen countless changes. "Veselka is a bulwark of consistency," says owner Tom Birchard (*pictured*). "The kind of place you can come and stay as long as you want."
144 2nd Avenue, NY 10003
+1 212 228 9682
veselka.com

Small wonder
—
Seek out this little gem for no-nonsense dining

And the fries are on their way, right?

⑬
Joseph Leonard, West Village
Unfussy dining

Unpretentious and relaxed, Joseph Leonard is a postage stamp-sized dining room and bar that is open all day during the week and for brunch at weekends. Gabriel Stulman and chef James McDuffee added the restaurant to their mini empire of West Village establishments in 2009 and came up with an unapologetically American menu.

Lunch features a grilled-cheese sandwich with gruyère, caraway, onions and mushrooms; when dinner time comes around there is a standout New York strip with bone marrow. A solid offering of seafood dishes and raw oysters rounds off the selection, while nighthawks will be pleased to find sustenance in a late-night menu featuring a smashed patty melt and chops dusted with Old Bay seasoning.
170 Waverly Place, NY 10014
+ 1 646 429 8383
josephleonard.com

⑭
Aria Wine Bar, West Village
Classic neighbourhood Italian

Set quietly on Perry Street in the West Village, this is a cosy post for quality wines and authentic Italian cooking. Simplicity is the watchword with white subway tiles covering the lengthy bar area, an ideal spot for parties of two to perch on wooden seats while tucking into shared plates. For larger groups, rustic wooden tables fill the rest of the candle-lit dining area. Sip a glass of red from a tumbler while plucking at gorgonzola-stuffed dates with speck, prosciutto-wrapped warm mozzarella with radicchio or pappardelle *pescatore*.
117 Perry Street, NY 10014
+1 212 242 4233

⑮
Luksus, Greenpoint
Nordic hideaway

Although it's a restaurant that is nearly invisible, this tasting-menu-only establishment shot to immediate success after opening its doors in Brooklyn's Greenpoint in 2013. "It's a good time to be in Greenpoint as it's changing," says Luksus partner and chef Daniel Burns. "It's still accessible from many parts of the city but it has a neighbourhood feel to it."

Situated behind a sliding door in the back of nouveau Danish beer hall Tørst, Luksus serves diners 13 elegant dishes: five to six snacks, main dishes and petit fours from a menu that changes every four to five weeks. Burns and his team are on view to guests, preparing plates such as bay scallop, *maitake* and silverberries or roasted squab with beetroot and salted plum purée.
615 Manhattan Avenue, NY 11222
+1 718 389 6034
luksusnyc.com

Bagel bakeries

01 Black Seed, Nolita: Since its launch in 2014, Black Seed on Elizabeth Street has raised the bar for bagel joints with an interior of sycamore, walnut and marble designed by Brooklyn property developer Home. Hand-rolled bagels are poached in honey water, baked in wood ovens and schmeared – as New Yorkers say it – with homemade spreads such as whitefish salad or beetroot-cured salmon.
blackseedbagels.com

02 Murray's Bagels, Chelsea: The bagels at Matt Pomerantz's much-loved establishment are made in-house and never toasted so the inside remains as soft as the outside is crisp. Try the sable special with spring-onion cream cheese, capers and tomatoes for an all-time favourite.
murraysbagelschelsea.com

03 Tompkins Square Bagels, East Village: See bagels being hand-rolled and kettle-boiled in the kitchen of this Tompkins Square Park hole-in-the-wall with a real neighbourhood feel. The range of spreads includes the sickly sweet Birthday Cake cream cheese; be warned, it isn't for every palate.
tompkinssquarebagels.com

⑱ Bar Boulud, Upper West Side
Broadway sommeliers

So you've ticked the culture box and traipsed round Lincoln Center; now you need a place to rest your feet. Bar Boulud is where you need to head. It's one of those places that knows what it does well and doesn't try to meddle with its bistro fodder.

Expect pâtés, steak frites and endive salads galore alongside some 500 wines in the restaurant's vaults, which holds one of the best selections of French vintages in the whole city. The chef and owner, Frenchman Daniel Boulud, also has an *épicerie* next door.
1900 Broadway, NY 10023
+1 212 595 0303
barboulud.com

Business lunches or dinners

01 Marea, Midtown: It may be a little glitzy but no one can argue with the Central Park location and the meticulously executed, fish-focused Italian menu.
marea-nyc.com

02 Lafayette, Nolita: High windows flood light into the elegant interior designed by Roman and Williams; a modern interpretation of the classic brasserie.
lafayetteny.com

03 Narcissa, East Village: The Standard hotel hosts this elegant spot, where Scandinavian style meets New American cuisine.
narcissarestaurant.com

04 The Odeon, Tribeca: The much-loved brasserie serves no-nonsense classics such as a herbed-chicken salad sandwich and steak tartare.
theodeonrestaurant.com

05 Il Buco, Noho: Rustic wooden tables adorn this Noho staple, offering simple Italian dishes in a pretension-free setting.
ilbuco.com

---

⑯ Shigure, Tribeca
For goodness: saké

This saké bar from Jiro Yamada and expert sommelier Takahiro Okada is ideal for post-work drinks and nibbles. A major draw is the expansive drinks list: sample 50 different kinds of saké (easy, now) from small Japanese distilleries. This includes rare tipples such as Junmai Daiginjo-shu; you can choose from more than a dozen types of *shochu* prepared by experts.

To balance all that booze there are *izakaya* bites such as potato-and-avocado salad, *shio koji* fried chicken or signature fried burdock-and-mizuna Shigure salad.
277 Church Street, NY 10013
+1 212 965 0200
sakebar-shigure.com

⑰ Estela, Nolita
Med in the mix

The accolades have been pouring in and yes, even Obama has dined here. But Estela isn't some fad, nor is it pretentious. The decor is simple to say the least: exposed brick (well, this is New York) and low-hanging lights create a laidback ambience. "We try to be as approachable as possible," says Uruguayan chef Ignacio Mattos, who previously worked at Il Buco. "Some of us come from a fine dining background but we want a bustling, fun place." The restaurant's melt-in-the-mouth burrata is arguably the star dish.
47 East Houston Street, NY 10012
+1 212 219 7693
estelanyc.com

Coffee stops

01 Budin, Greenpoint:
Started by three friends
with Nordic ancestry,
Budin's wood-heavy
interior hosts a diverse
selection of Scandinavian
coffees and speciality
items from Europe's
northern latitudes. Many
offerings are exclusive
to Budin – ask for the
Good Life blend, which
is roasted in Helsinki.
budin-nyc.com

**02 Irving Farm, Lower East
Side:** There is a polish
to the area that might
turn some people off;
fortunately, Irving Farm
pours a bit of upstate
grit into the shiny mugs
of those who live here.
Exceptional coffees are
roasted on a sprawling
farm north of the city.
Many of the pastries are
baked in-house and the
food menu means you
can easily spend an hour
or two here.
irvingfarm.com

**03 Gasoline Alley Coffee,
Noho:** Something in the
design of this cubbyhole-
sized shop and the brew
it serves keeps us coming
back. The stripped-down
menu indicates that those
in charge aren't about
fluff; benches outside
are a great places to
people-watch.
gasolinealleycoffee.com

⑲
Café Mogador, Williamsburg
North African nourishment

The undisputed place to eat
Moroccan food in New York,
Mogador opened its first branch in
the East Village in 1983 and then in
Williamsburg in 2012. An unfussy
family-run restaurant, its decor is
homely (think wooden tables and
black-and-white framed photos on
the walls). The food is simple but
delicious and reasonably priced (a
rarity in New York). We particularly
like the chicken *bastilla*: shredded
organic chicken with almonds,
egg, herbs and spices inside a light
pastry. Try to bag a table in the
plant-filled conservatory out back.
*133 Wythe Avenue, NY 11211
+1 718 486 9222
cafemogador.com*

⑳
Jack's Wife Freda, West Village
Low-key dining

Jack's Wife Freda opened its second iteration in late 2014 on charming Carmine Street. The café's menu features an all-day selection of simple yet delicious dishes, including a fresh take on Israeli *shakshuka* and the Madame Freda sandwich with duck prosciutto and cheddar béchamel. Rustic hospitality is everything here. "I like a place that is for everybody," says Dean Jankelowitz, who founded the café with his wife Maya. "Young or old, families: everybody is welcome."
50 Carmine Street, NY 10014
+ 1 646 669 9888
jackswifefreda.com

㉑
Fort Defiance, Red Hook
Healthy attitude

If there is an adjective to describe the people of Brooklyn's Red Hook it's "defiant". A victim of Hurricane Sandy flooding in 2012, this corner of New York has time and again defied the odds and it's no mystery why local restaurateurs might name a place Fort Defiance. Salads of locally sourced produce and main dishes of meat and fish hint at comfort food but aspire to be the right amount of healthy. On

Thursday nights the Sunken Harbor Club takes over the bar with a tropical *tiki* theme, even in the dead of winter. Defiant, indeed.
365 Van Brunt Street, NY 11231
+ 1 347 453 6672
fortdefiancebrooklyn.com

㉒
Red Rooster, Harlem
Harlem showstopper

This restaurant is named after a nearby legendary speakeasy. Regulars on the soul food-inspired menu include shrimp and grits, lobster mac'n'cheese and blackened catfish. Another major draw is the live music: jazz on Sundays, "unplugged" on Mondays and soul on Thursdays.
310 Lenox Avenue, NY 10027
+ 1 212 792 9001
redroosterharlem.com

Essex Street Market

This hodgepodge of 20 independent sellers is one of the best-kept secrets in the city. Sure, the neighbours know but the Lower East Side (the 'hood in which the market sits) wasn't always a desirable place to go shopping for supplies. Still, many longstanding specialist food sellers – and a few new arrivals – mean you can find just about anything you'd want for a meal here. From fresh-baked French breads to fine local meats, the products within the market are top drawer (think about stopping by for a picnic on a walk to the East River).
essexstreetmarket.com

01 Pain d'Avignon: The perfect place to start a market tour; the bakery's wall of fresh bread is best perused early morning.
paindavignon-nyc.com
02 Saxelby Cheesemongers: One of a few places to find cheese but this one tops them all.
saxelbycheese.com
03 Shopsin's: The servers at this diner are not the most polite people you'll meet in the city (they're actually quite proud of that) but they make a mean macaroni-cheese pancake. Don't question it, just order it.
shopsins.com

(23)
Peasant, Nolita
Simple pleasures

Once it was easy to go wrong when
looking for rustic Italian food in
Little Italy. But Frank DeCarlo
changed things when he opened
Peasant in 1999, bringing a taste
of the real Italy to the area. With
exposed brick walls and long
wooden tables, Peasant is like
stepping into a medieval dining
room, albeit a chic one. The pan-
Italian menu is big on flavour and
generous in size. A wood-fired oven
is the focal point for the space and
the cooking: dishes such as grilled
sea bream or whole roast suckling
pig are infused with its flavour.
194 Elizabeth Street, NY 10012
+ 1 212 965 9511
peasantnyc.com

Full service
—
Large groups
can opt for
the tasting
menu

Oyster bars

01 Grand Central Oyster
Bar, Midtown: The
grandfather of New York
oyster bars is housed
within the beaux arts
confines of Grand Central
Station, nestled amid
the splendour of its
concave roof and wooden
panelling. The vast menu
talks you through the size,
characteristics and origin
of the oysters sourced
along the Atlantic coast
from Rhode Island to
Nova Scotia.
oysterbarny.com

02 Maison Premiere,
Williamsburg: Two
nondescript doors,
conspicuously high
windows and a basic
sign are the only clues
to Maison Premiere's
existence. Walk through
that door though and you
discover a horseshoe bar
and a small fireplace. The
decor is something of a
step back in time, as are
the bartenders dressed
in trousers and braces.
It's a little precious but
remember you're here for
the seafood – among the
freshest we've found in
New York.
maisonpremiere.com

03 Mermaid Inn, East
Village: Once a humble
seafood shack, the
Mermaid now boasts
three venues but has
managed to keep hold
of the bustle and charm
that made it so popular to
start with. The premise is
simple but effective with
cut-price oysters during
the daily two-hour happy
hour (17.00 to 19.00;
all night in Greenwich
Village on Mondays). The
Mermaid Inn also does
a mean lobster roll and
grilled New England hake.
themermaidnyc.com

③
Café Colette, Williamsburg
Creative corner

This is where the beautiful people of Williamsburg come out to play, flocking to this New American bistro for rustic, creative food. Take a seat in the greenhouse garden, prop up the zinc-covered bar or, for maximum people-watching potential, claim one of the tables that line the façade. Brunch options include poached eggs with roasted squash and hearty mains feature butter-bean-and-kale stew with grilled sourdough. It's all washed down with one (or indeed several) of Colette's classic cocktails with a twist.
79 Berry Street, NY 11249
+ 1 379 599 1381
cafe-colette.com

① Buvette, West Village
European sophistication

Opened by American chef Jody Williams but the food is very much rooted in Gallic traditions. Bringing a little of the "small plate" concept that is popular in Europe, the menu at Buvette – worth a visit for its design alone – is about rustic French food and wine with a West Village twist.

The welcoming environment makes for an excellent weekend brunch pit-stop: go simple with a croissant and jam washed down with a café au lait and freshly squeezed orange juice or all-out NYC with eggs and a cocktail.
42 Grove Street, NY 10014
+ 1 212 255 3590
newyork.ilovebuvette.com

② Café Cluny, West Village
Et voilà

Brunch doesn't always have to be a blow-out (although it can feel that way in New York), which is where this French-influenced establishment in the West Village steps in. Waiters in striped shirts can serve you homemade granola should you wish to sidestep the eggs; the franglais frisée salad aux lardons is also a classic. If you venture later in the day, the three-course prix-fixe dinner is a winner, preferably accompanied by a bottle of riesling. Check out the portraits above the window of patrons drawn by a Central Park artist.
284 West 12th Street, NY 10014
+ 1 212 255 6900
cafecluny.com

The brunch craze is positively out of control in New York: it goes all weekend from early morning until evening. From truffled eggs to champagne-soaked berries, the opulence can be staggering. But it is a lot of fun.

Drinks
Spirit of the city

1

The Raines Law Room,
Flatiron District
Atmospheric speakeasy

Opened in 2009, The Raines Law
Room is a sophisticated cocktail
lounge that takes a step back
in time to a key moment in US
history: the lead-up to prohibition.
The name itself references an 1896
New York state law that banned
alcohol sales on Sundays, leading
establishments to find innovative
ways to flout the rules.

As a reminder of bygone years,
a host continues to greet guests
from behind a plain, lacquered
black door, curtly refusing entry if
the lounge is over capacity. Once
inside, the service is attentive and
the decor is 1920s-inspired, with
vast chandeliers, plush Chesterfield
seating and dim lighting.
48 West 17th Street, NY 10011
raineslawroom.com

I call this cocktail Bottle of Red to Myself

2

Hotel Delmano, Williamsburg
Innovative mixers

With its curved bar, chandeliers and
tarnished mirrors, Hotel Delmano
has an elegantly dishevelled feel,
as if you're stepping into another
era. Friendly staff will find you a
cosy nook in one of two adjoining
rooms or street-side tables during
warmer months. The focus is on
imaginative, grown-up cocktails
such as the cheekily named San
Francisco handshake (thyme-
infused gin, St Germain, lemon
and Fernet Branca). There's also
a raw-oyster and seafood bar,
charcuterie and extensive wine list
packed with local producers.
82 Berry Street, NY 11211
+1 718 387 1945
hoteldelmano.com

Classic bars

01 King Cole Bar, Midtown:
Located inside the St
Regis Hotel, the King
Cole Bar is where the Red
Snapper was invented
in 1934, known today as
the Bloody Mary. That
name was too risqué for
the debonair St Regis
crowd back then, drinking
beneath Maxfield Parrish's
massive painting "Old
King Cole". The picture
still dominates the dimly
lit room and the drink is
still on the menu under its
original moniker – enjoy a
Red Snapper and soak up
the timeless atmosphere.
kingcolebar.com

02 Bemelmans, Upper East
Side: No establishment
oozes old New York
style like Bemelmans at
the Carlyle Hotel. At its
founding in 1947, Ludwig
Bemelmans – creator
of the *Madeline* picture
books and a Carlyle
regular – painted the
colourful murals with
figures that might have
leaped from his stories.
Not a night passes
without live music: piano
until 21.00 and jazz until
midnight. Every Monday,
Woody Allen plays clarinet
next door at Café Carlyle.
rosewoodhotels.com

03 The Campbell
Apartment, Midtown:
Set inside Grand Central
station, this hideaway is a
step back in time. Outside
of commuting hours,
imbibing in this former
office of 1920s financier
John W Campbell feels
like drinking in a sanctuary,
all subtly lit by leaded
windows that let in a soft
glow. We recommend the
Kentucky Ginger (bourbon,
ginger liqueur, rosemary
and lemon) as a nightcap.
hospitalityholdings.com

Rooftop bars

01 The Ides Bar, Wythe Hotel, Williamsburg: One of the best places to pause and take in your surroundings with a well-mixed drink from its cocktail list.
wythehotel.com

02 Gallow Green, Chelsea: The rooftop bar of the fictional McKittrick Hotel, part of *Sleep No More*'s immersive theatre experience, is open to the public and is a beautiful green space. It transforms into a warming indoor lodge in winter.
m.mckittrickhotel.com/ gallowgreen

03 Northern Territory, Greenpoint: Laidback wooden seating, summer barbecues and views over Brooklyn and Manhattan; this is also one rooftop bar where you might actually get a seat.
northernterritorybk.com

04 Top of the Standard and Le Bain, Meatpacking District: André Balazs's iconic hotel has become an established part of city nightlife and offers a range of eating and drinking options. But for the real action you need to move on up. The Top of the Standard (formerly known as The Boom Boom Room) is an intimate space with knockout views of Manhattan and the Hudson River. Alternatively, try penthouse discotheque and adjoining rooftop bar Le Bain, which boasts equally exceptional views and, during the summer months, a dancefloor and a hot tub. Subtle it is not; a lot of fun it most certainly is.
standardhotels.com

(4)

The Nomad Bar, Nomad
Accessible grandeur

If you can't get a table at the Nomad restaurant (*see page 23*), its bar evokes a similar feeling of opulence, only on a bigger, brasher scale. Accessible from West 28th Street or the hotel's library bar, it's overtly masculine in feel with mahogany-lined walls, green-leather booths and a mirrored bar that rises up into a dramatic two-storey space. Alongside the selection of cocktail classics, "Cocktail Explosions" are on offer for groups. The food menu is more keenly priced and accessible than that of the hotel restaurant.
10 West 28th Street, NY 10001
+1 212 796 1500
thenomadhotel.com

(3)

The Blue Ribbon Bar, West Village
Early-evening kickstarter

The Downing Street Bar is just across the street from the famous Blue Ribbon Bakery restaurant in the West Village. That establishment is worth a visit in itself but its sister bar is an excellent place to start the night. The white-oak panelled space is moodily lit and you can usually find a perch at the marble bar or at one of the tables around the French-limestone floor. The cocktail menu is extensive but the olives and cheeses demand a good red – and the wine list doesn't lack for options, particularly from California and Piedmont.
34 Downing Street, NY 10014
+1 212 691 0404
blueribbonrestaurants.com

(5)

Employees Only, West Village
Service with style

Launched in 2004, Employees Only upholds the time-honoured traditions of New York speakeasies: bartenders in smart jackets and perfectly mixed drinks, including an extensive whiskey menu served from the long, curvy bar. Food favourites include the roast chicken and the whole-wheat spaghetti; a reservation is worth the trouble if you want a table in the dining room. The bar's own tasty Bloody Mary mixer and grenadine is also a hit. Co-founder Dushan Zaric insists food, decor, service and drinks should blend seamlessly.
510 Hudson Street, NY 10014
+1 212 242 3021
employeesonlynyc.com

Retail
—— Store crazy

From small Soho outlets to the temples of commerce on Fifth Avenue, this is a city built for retail. As you'd expect from a megapolis with so much fashion-industry clout, the world's powerhouse brands all have flagships here, many of them design sanctuaries in their own right. Be sure to check out some of the department store windows too, if we're talking about aesthetics.

There are always surprises in this city that constantly strives to be bigger and bolder. You can wear anything you want and you can equally find whatever you want, be it Czech pencils from McNally Jackson Store or a well-made T-shirt from James Perse. Oh, and we wouldn't want you to forget the Monocle shop in the West Village while you're at it.

① Modern Anthology, Dumbo
Gentleman's relish

In the diminutive Dumbo neighbourhood, Modern Anthology is a refuge from the construction rumble and phone chatter of techies on cigarette breaks. The shop sells one-off furniture pieces and objects for the tasteful gentleman, such as a handmade coffee table using hardwoods from defunct telephone poles and railway sleepers. The clothing pick is just as impressive, with brands including Raleigh Denim and Todd Snyder. You'll also find men's accessories and grooming products.
*68 Jay Street, NY 11201
+1 718 522 3020
modernanthology.com*

Oh, now don't you look really rather fetching

Project No 8, Lower East Side
Limited-edition specialists

Situated on the edge of the Lower East Side, Project No 8 opened its doors in 2009, the brainchild of husband-and-wife team Brian Janusiak and Elizabeth Beer. After forming design studio Various Projects in 2005 they decided to branch into retail. Concrete flooring and white walls intentionally provide a gallery-like space that showcases menswear pieces, accessories and one-off collaborations. In-house products by Various Projects, such as key tags and a knitted baby pigeon, are also on offer.
38 Orchard Street, NY 10002
+ 1 212 925 5599
projectno8.com

Fivestory, Upper East Side
Continental-style boutique

With its marble floors and selection of fashion, accessories and home decor, this concept shop located in a traditional townhouse was designed to rival Colette in Paris and Milan's 10 Corso Como. Founder Claire Distenfeld has given Fivestory an intimate feel where dresses, shoes and jewellery are displayed like artwork. From sunglasses by Oliver Peoples and handbags by Olympia Le-Tan to Narciso Rodriguez couture, Fivestory is about discovering adventurous combinations, one-off gems and up-and-coming brands.
18 East 69th Street, NY 10065
+ 1 212 288 1338
fivestoryny.com

Steven Alan Annex, Chelsea
The art of outfitting

Nestled between art galleries, this spacious, industrial-style shop sells everything from quality brogues and fitted blazers to tasteful home goods – oh, and a homemade courgette relish. Alan, an investor in Detroit's Shinola, features an eponymous "Collection" alongside brands such as Acne and APC, as well as smaller designers including Nili Lotan. Staff are friendly without being overbearing and there's always good music on the hi-fi. There is another Annex on Franklin Street and two shops in Brooklyn.
140 10th Avenue, NY 10011
+ 1 646 664 0606
stevenalan.com

6

Maison Kitsuné, Nomad
Culture clash

Paris-based brand Maison Kitsuné
is the brainchild of Gildas Loaëc,
Daft Punk's ex-manager, and
fashion designer Masaya Kuroki.
Meaning "fox with many faces" in
Japanese, Kitsuné offers a suitably
eclectic mix of fashion and music.
. The New York outpost (the only
one in North America) can be
found at The Nomad Hotel (*see
page 23*) where, alongside its own
clothing range, Kitsuné carries
like-minded brands such as
Alexander Olch and Aesop. Its
music compilations, available on
CD and vinyl, never disappoint.
1170 Broadway, NY 10001
+1 212 481 6010
shop.kitsune.fr

⑤
Monocle Shop, West Village
Our embassy in New York

Every item in our NY shop – from
acrylic canvas carry-on bags to
brass-plated paperweights – aspires
to bring harmony to your hectic life
and keep you looking good, too.
A series of Comme des Garçons-
produced unisex fragrances (one
of which evokes a Japanese *hinoki*
soaking tub) is a hit among
travellers looking to freshen up
before a night on the town, while
new items previewed each month
online and in the magazine are
snapped up almost as quickly as
they're unpacked from the box. Look
out for our Voyage clothing line.
535 Hudson Street, NY 10014
+1 212 229 1120
monocle.com

Perfect picks

01 Leather bags by Want Les
Essentiels de la Vie
02 Chunky-knit jumper by
Kitsuné Paris
03 Bow ties by Alexander Olch
04 Travel kit by Flouzen x
Kitsuné Paris
05 Sunglasses by Oliver
Peoples x Kitsuné Paris

Proud heritage
—
The building has previously housed design schools

⑦
Dover Street Market, Murray Hill
One-stop concept shop

A beaux arts mansion built in 1909 houses Rei Kawakubo's visionary multibrand shop, a third outpost (following London and Tokyo) that focuses on the avant garde and the unusual. Each of the shop's seven floors is uniquely designed and intermixed with artist installations such as the floor-to-ceiling column covered in knitting by artist Magda Sayeg and meticulously selected brands including Prada, Sacai and JW Anderson.

The shop goes through a biannual transformation of its space in January and July, which it uses to refresh brand offerings and rethink its creative focus. After a morning of shopping you can enjoy a cup of organic rooibos tea and *kuri* squash quiche at Rose Bakery (a branch of the famed Paris bakers in the French capital's Marais Nord) on the ground floor.
160 Lexington Avenue, NY 10016
+1 646 837 7750
newyork.doverstreetmarket.com

Wrist action
—
Look out for Shinola's striking watch range

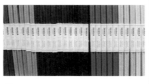

① **The Primary Essentials, Boerum Hill**
Simple style

Lauren Snyder's small but perfectly formed store focuses on home-and-beauty niche items sourced from small-scale designers and artisans. An experienced fashion stylist, Snyder trained as an interior designer and opened her shop in 2013. The many designers she has picked out offer practical creations with an aesthetic that is both unfussy and easy on the eye. While there is plenty in store to impress, our favourites at The Primary Essentials include Le Feu de l'Eau candles and traditional handspun *khadi* textiles from Auntie Oti.
372 Atlantic Avenue, NY 11217
+1 718 522 1804
theprimaryessentials.com

⑧ Shinola, Tribeca
Pioneer of creativity

The story of Detroit's creative resurgence has been well documented following its bankruptcy in 2013 but no one embodies it quite like Shinola. The company actually bought the name from the shoe-polish brand established in Detroit in 1907 but the new premise is very different: masterly crafted "Made in America" watches, leather goods and bicycles.

Shinola's Rockwell Group-designed Tribeca flagship evokes a golden age of Detroit with black-and-white photos of city characters. In need of a caffeine fix before shopping? In-house The Smile Café (which you pass through on the way to the main shop) is on hand to serve you before you decide on a handmade, individually numbered timepiece.
177 Franklin Street, NY 10013
+1 917 728 3000
shinola.com

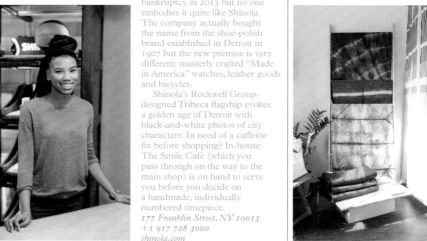

Ⓐ
ABC Carpet & Home,
Flatiron District
Luxe touch

Spanning six floors, ABC Carpet &
Home is a shop to enjoy getting lost
in. It boasts six-metre-high ceilings
with no dividing walls in order to
showcase its carpets and is known
for outstanding luxury rugs. "I
don't think there is another space in
the city that has this," says company
vice-chairman Graham Head.

Sure, a carpet won't fit in your
carry-on but you can have it
delivered to your house. Plus there
is an array of jewellery, cosmetics
ceramics and decorations by the
likes of Tom Dixon and Cappellini.
888 Broadway, NY 10003
+ 1 212 473 3000
abchome.com

Ⓑ
Still House, East Village
Design showcase

Half way between shop and gallery,
Still House celebrates clever
design and quality materials and
has become the place to discover
emerging design talent from the
US, Japan and Scandinavia. A
thoughtful selection of homeware
and stationery is displayed in
equally considered and welcoming
surroundings, all designed by
founder Urte Tylaite. The shop
sells its own range of contemporary
jewellery, too: delicate and beautiful
geometric pieces in silver and gold,
often with pleasingly subtle and
surprising twists.
117 East 7th Street, NY 10009
+ 1 212 539 0200
stillhousenyc.com

Ⓓ
Michele Varian, Soho
Personal touch

Expect to find both familiar and
playful accessories for the home at
this Crosby Street establishment.
The airy, wooded space is filled
with ceramics, linens, artwork
and jewellery – carefully chosen
merchandise that makes a trip
there feel like sifting through a
treasure trove. Michele Varian's
space is home to pieces from
more than 100 designers, most of
them from the US. Her occasional
"Downstairs with Michele Varian"
pop-up shop creates an accessible
platform to connect New York with
vendors in other cities in the US.
27 Howard Street, NY 10013
+1 212 343 0033
michelevarian.com

BDDW, Soho
One-man show

The skillfully fashioned items in this bright, spacious Crosby Street showroom are the handiwork of owner Tyler Hays, a painter, sculptor and furniture maker. Everything in this airy Soho shop – from the toddler-sized moccasins to the American Holly and bronze credenzas – is meticulously made but nothing feels too precious.

The pieces (we like the walnut-slab coffee table and the hanging leather mirrors) are all handmade in Hays' Philadelphia workshop. The shop also includes his own line of ceramics.

Hays – who also practises archery in the space on occasion – has his fingers in many pies. He has bought a shop in Lostine, Oregon, that is more than 100 years old and has inspired a range of products from homeware to fashion. The man never stops.
5 Crosby Street, NY 10013
+1 212 625 1230
bddw.com

(7)
The Future Perfect, Noho
Visionary curation

Noho-based The Future Perfect, which sells designer furniture, looks like a cross between a modern art gallery and a New York-loft living room. Just off Bowery and signposted in 1980s neon, it offers high-end design that draws a savvy clientele. When David Alhadeff launched the brand in Brooklyn in 2003 he decided to source his furniture from lesser-known local workshops and over the years, despite expanding The Future Perfect's range, he hasn't lost sight of helping up-and-coming talent.

Nowadays you'll find woodwork from Portugal and upholstery from the UK alongside tables and lights from New York: think stone coffee tables, sparse but comfortable leather sofas and Picasso-esque glass vases.
55 Great Jones Street, NY 10012
+1 877 388 7373
thefutureperfect.com

(5)
Nalata Nalata, East Village
Minimal mantra

Canadian designers Stevenson Aung and Angélique Chmielewski founded Nalata Nalata in 2012 to showcase the work of fellow craftsman and friends.

Once online-only, the retailer opened a physical space in 2014. The store is elegantly understated with white-oak cabinets, shelves and a slatted ceiling. "We wanted the shop to act as a backdrop to the products, so when it came to the build we kept with a minimal aesthetic," says Aung. Nalata Nalata also launched a namesake line along with its expansion.
2 Extra Place, NY 10003
+1 212 228 1030
nalatanalata.com

Aung and Chmielewski's favourite shops in New York:

01 Green Fingers: The Noho outpost of the Japanese flower shop chain.
greenfingersnyc.com

02 Mast Books: Rare book shop in East Village.
mastbooks.com

03 Shibui: Antiques warehouse shop in Dumbo.
shibui.com

04 Smooch: For fine organic coffee, food and wine.
smoochorganic.com

05 Fabulous Fanny's: Great vintage finds in LES.
fabulousfannys.com

Menswear
Wardrobe renewal

①

Saturdays Surf NYC, Soho
Tailored beachwear

Manhattan may not be an obvious birthplace for a surf brand but Saturdays is bringing a dose of laidback Californian cool to the metropolis regardless. Co-founded by a trio of big-wave lovers in 2009, Saturdays makes high-quality men's clothing with a modern, minimal aesthetic and a closer attention to cut than traditional surfwear.

Its strong identity is evident throughout, from the simple shop interiors to the brand's magazine. With an in-house café serving La Colombe coffee, Saturdays' two New York locations have become a regular hangout for city surfers.
31 Crosby Street, NY 10013
+1 212 966 7873
saturdaysnyc.com

Wave riders
—
Rockaway Beach boasts two surfing spots

②
Brooklyn Tailors, Williamsburg
Custom fitters

Californians Daniel and Brenna
Lewis started their tailoring
business out of their Clinton
Hill apartment in 2007. Since
then the name has become
synonymous with sharp, detailed
tailoring as the company went
on to launch a ready-to-wear
collection in 2011 from its
retail space in Williamsburg.
There you can find a modern
collection of shirting, suits,
trousers and ties. If you're
after a fitting, the shop happily
takes walk-ins or will set
up private appointments.
358 Grand Street, NY 11211
+ 1 347 799 1646
brooklyntailors.net

③
CHCM, Noho
Pop-up passion

Minutes away from the fast-
fashion chain stores of Soho, CHCM
was opened by former product
designer Sweetu Patel in 2010. The
name originally stood for Clinton
Hill Classic Menswear, the online
retail venture he launched from
his Brooklyn home. After a few
successful pop-ups, Patel opened
a multibrand outlet but now stocks
solely the in-house line.

The clothes range from woollen
jackets to wax-quilted trenches that
are "made for us by the original
manufacturers we started selling
years ago", says Patel.
2 Bond Street, NY 10012
+1 212 673 8601
chcmshop.com

④
James Perse, Soho
Tactile tees and more

LA-based James Perse offers
a relaxed yet elegant take on
West Coast living with a range
that encompasses everything
from beachwear and blankets to
beautifully crafted furniture. For
active souls there's Yosemite: a slick
performance clothing line of sweats
and shorts. However the ultra-soft
T-shirts remain at the heart of the
brand's collections and come in
a range of soothing earthy tones,
designed to take you from poolside
to restaurant table.

If you're looking to bring a little
Californian cool to your stay on
the East Coast, New York is home
to four Perse boutiques, including
smaller, separate men's and
women's shops in the West Village.
But to fully appreciate the brand's
relaxed style, head to this larger
Soho location on Mercer Street.
60 Mercer Street, NY 10013
+1 212 334 3501
jamesperse.com

Will
this
count
as
carry-
on?

⑤
J.Crew Liquor Store, Tribeca
Renewed edge

The J.Crew men's shop occupies
an 1825 landmarked townhouse
that was once the Tribeca Tavern.
Here you can browse through the
brand's best menswear offerings,
alongside favourite picks from the
likes of Billykirk, Private White
VC and Red Wing boots – as well
as some vintage finds. The space
is small but inviting with original
detailing such as a whitewashed
fireplace and original bar top where
you can find the staff manning
the till. A few shelves of premium
liquor are evident but ask for a
glass and see how far it gets you.
235 West Broadway, NY 10013
+1 212 226 5476
jcrew.com

Perfect picks

01 Hand-sewn derbies by Engineered Garments x Tricker's
02 Logger jacket by Needles
03 Incense by Senses
04 Jumper by South2 West8
05 *The Green Soccer Journal*

Ⓖ
Carson Street Clothiers, Soho
Global blend

"We wanted to build a home base for men of discerning taste; a place where they simply enjoyed being," says Carson Street Clothiers co-founder Brian Trunzo, who together with business partner Matt Breen (*both pictured, Trunzo on left*) quit corporate law to launch their retail venture.

Chesterfield couches bring a cosy touch to the sleek shop, which stocks brands ranging from heritage to runway, including Mackintosh, Patrik Ervell, Tomorrowland, Mismo and Lemaire. "It's the mixing and matching, the cross-section, that we find most interesting," says Trunzo. "New York style is a melting pot of every aesthetic: mid-century modern, rustic Americana, minimalist. We've settled on calling the blending of these styles 'sophisticated industrial'."
63 Crosby Street, NY 10012
+1 212 925 2627
carsonstreetclothiers.com

Ⓖ
Nepenthes NY, Garment District
Subtle sophistication

Nepenthes NY, the first international outpost of the Japanese retailer, is housed in an old sewing-machine shop and offers a collection of clothing and accessories from in-house brands such as South2 West8 and Needles. Naturally there's also Nepenthes' leading in-house brand Engineered Garments, designed and manufactured four blocks away. "Much of what we make or collaborate on is a new and fun but subtle approach to a classic style," says founder Keizo Shimizu, who opened the New York branch in 2010.
307 West 38th Street, NY 10018
+1 212 643 9540
nepenthesny.com

Ⓖ
Gentry, Williamsburg
Rock' n'roll stars

Williamsburg's clothing retailer Gentry goes beyond what the name of the shops suggests: it is a treasure trove of urban necessities drawn from European and Japanese brands. Borsalino hats, scarves and ties by Drake's, clothes from Ts(s) and knits by SNS Herning are among the most popular items.

Heavy rock is the soundtrack here, played just loudly enough to serve as a reminder of what this place is all about: the latest city fashion delivered in a manner that only New York can pull off.
109 South 5th Street, NY 11249
+1 718 384 8585
gentrynyc.com

What's in a name?
—
Odin is the father of the gods in Norse mythology

⑨
Odin, Soho
Man's best friend

There are three Odin shops in Manhattan: the original East Village location, a newer outpost in West Village and the flagship in Soho, all fitted out to give the feel of a modern gentleman's club. A one-stop shop for the style-conscious man, they cover everything from casual basics to sharp tailoring and the service is excellent.

Homegrown brands such as Thom Browne, Engineered Garments and Alex Mill are joined by cult Japanese and Swedish imports including Junya Watanabe and Acne. They have an extensive range of accessories too, including Odin's in-house line of fragrances, wallets and bags from Comme des Garçons and Want les Essentiels de la Vie's debut footwear collection, alongside a great selection of sunglasses and skincare.
199 Lafayette Street, NY 10012
+1 212 966 0026
odinnewyork.com

Why thank you kind officer – much obliged

① Bird, Williamsburg
Green goddess

Bird has been called "the queen of Brooklyn retail" and owner Jennifer Mankins can be credited at least in part for crystallising the Brooklyn look in her three boutiques dotted around the New York borough. Her flagship shop in Williamsburg was designed by the Norwegian architect Ole Sondreson and is the first nationally certified green retail store in the city. Featured brands include APC, Isabel Marant and Comme des Garçons, but we recommend lesser-known names such as Black Crane for all of your Japanese minimalist clothing needs or the Korean designer Yune Ho for warm and constructed women's pieces. Bird also has a great menswear selection, as well as a wide range of jewellery and accessories.
203 Grand Street, NY 11211
+1 718 388 1655
shopbird.com

Glorious past
—
Mankins' CV includes head buyer at Steven Alan

② Rachel Comey, Soho
Fantastic footwear

Situated behind the bustle of Broadway on quiet Crosby Street, Rachel Comey's signature shop feels like a calm sanctuary. The single-storey building – a former mechanic's garage – was transformed by Comey and her partner Sean Carmody, along with architect Elizabeth Roberts and interior designer Charles de Lisle. A concrete-stone slab sits in the centre, showing off Comey's signature footwear.

The designer, who started in menswear at the launch of her New York label in 2001, now focuses on her urban and chic women's collection, which is carefully displayed on brass racks against the shop's white stucco walls. With Comey's studio situated in nearby Noho and her home just steps away, the designer's presence is never too far from the serene space.
*95 Crosby Street, NY 10012
+1 212 334 0455
rachelcomey.com*

Time to order more shopping bags

③
Maryam Nassir Zadeh,
Lower East Side
Worldly charm

This polished women's boutique
sits just above Chinatown in a lush,
all-white space decked out with
palm trees, crystals and a set of
high-backed wicker garden chairs
– perfect for worn-out shoppers in
need of a rest. Co-owner Maryam
Nassir Zadeh has an eye for
vintage-inspired, Parisian-feeling
pieces and she travels the globe
scouting young designers. The
overall aesthetic is functional
without sacrificing flair: silk brocade
jackets blend in with kaftan-esque
dresses designed by the owner.
123 Norfolk Street, NY 10002
+1 212 673 6405
mnzstore.com

**Perfect
picks**
—
01 Maryam Nassir Zadeh's
in-house shoe line
02 Knitwear by Lauren
Manoogian
03 Leather jackets by Acne
04 Dresses from Étoile
Isabel Marant
05 Tote by Rochas

④
Pas de Deux, East Village
Curated elegance

Chequered marble floors,
chandeliers, floral bouquets and
rows of designer dresses instil a
Parisian flair in this East Village
boutique that opened next door
to sister brand Odin in 2008. The
narrow space – which resembles a
fantasy walk-in wardrobe – is lined
with shelves showcasing ensembles
by the likes of Isabel Marant Étoile
and Alexander Wang interspersed
with jewellery by Gabriela Artigas
and shoes by Dieppa Restrepo. It
is all selected by co-owners Eddy
Chai and Paul Birardi to provide
elegant cocktail and casualwear.
328 East 11th Street, NY 10003
+1 212 475 0075
pasdedeuxny.com

⑤
Creatures of Comfort, Nolita
Smart and chic

After an initial five years in Los
Angeles, Creatures of Comfort
founder Jade Lai transported her
boutique to the East Coast in 2010.
Situated on stylish Mulberry Street
in Nolita, Lai brings an extended
selection of smart brands such as
Tokyo's Cosmic Wonder and LA's
Band of Outsiders. Exposed brick
walls, scuffed wooden floors and
tall windows are a fitting backdrop
to the well-made, elegant designs
on the racks. The bright and airy
space, once an NYPD precinct
building, is also home to the in-house
Creatures of Comfort collection.
205 Mulberry Street, NY 10012
+1 212 925 1005
creaturesofcomfort.us

Department stores
Stately selections

01 Barneys, Midtown:
First established in 1923
as a menswear shop on
Manhattan's west side,
Barneys' original slogan was
"For the man who knows".
The venture maintained this
conspiratorial coda as it
expanded into womenswear
in the 1970s, becoming a
counterpoint to the uptown
retailers with an edgy mix
of younger designers and
high-end luxury.
    Today, the department
store – now found on
Madison Avenue – maintains
its reputation as an arbiter of
haute-fashion and brand
collaborations, as well as
featuring established labels
such as Lanvin and Prada.
The space has nine storeys
of high-end brands including
its Emerging Designer
floors, which have built the
reputation of young talent
such as En Noir and Public
School. The recently
renovated fifth floor is
dedicated to men's and
women's shoes – arguably
the most luxurious place in
the city to rest your feet
while shopping.
barneys.com

02 Bergdorf Goodman,
Midtown: Bergdorf
Goodman opened in 1899
and was originally located in
the Flatiron District before
moving to its current Fifth
Avenue location. It's one of
those shops that, regardless
of the glitz and pomp, is
typically New York: a big
name that has managed to
maintain some of the charm
and fashion of the golden
age of the city, despite its
global repute and the hordes
of tourists who frequent it.
    Occupying a historic
townhouse – the top floor
was once the residence of
the Bergdorf family – it has
played a major part in New
York changing fashions. The
brands here are all big name
(Gucci, Prada, Dior et al) and
being at Bergdorf means
being part of the history of
how the city dresses itself
(the retailer's backing can
help make or break a brand).
With its window displays
elevated to a high artform
(especially at Christmas) by
resident window dresser
David Hoey, no one does
luxury retail quite like
Bergdorf Goodman.
bergdorfgoodman.com

Bookshops
Top reads

①

McNally Jackson, Nolita
Book and stationery master

McNally Jackson Books captures a golden age of bookshops: a refined selection that includes art, photography and graphic design alongside a small DVD selection, set over two floors. Look out for the "espresso" book machine – a gizmo that can print a self-published book in six minutes (at a cost).

Around the corner, McNally Jackson Store: Goods for the Study is a beacon of good taste. Squeezed into a tiny space is a collection of stationery, paper, notebooks, pens and everything else you need to decorate the perfect office. Think the finest French ink from J Herbin or pens and pencils from Czech company Koh-i-Noor Hardtmuth.
Books: 52 Prince Street, NY 10012
+1 212 274 1160
mcnallyjackson.com;
Stationery: 234 Mulberry Street,
NY 10012
+1 212 219 2789
mcnallyjacksonstore.com

Speedy service
—
Delivery by bicycle is offered in Manhattan

Four more

01 Kinokuniya Bookstore, Midtown: Designed to provide the city's Japanese diaspora with books and magazines from home, Kinokuniya also wants to introduce Japanese culture abroad. The 20,000 book titles are arranged not by language but by category. In the basement the selection of stationery and hard-to-find magazines is unequalled in the city.
kinokuniya.com

02 Idlewild Books, Flatiron District: One of the last bookshops in the country dedicated to travel, from global guides and travelogues to travel-related fiction. Founded in 2008 by a former UN press officer, Idlewild has also built a reputation as a provider of language classes taught by native speakers. Also check out the Brooklyn store opened in Cobble Hill in 2012.
idlewildbooks.com

03 Greenlight Bookstore, Brooklyn: A beautiful space surrounded by bars and restaurants with a real neighbourhood feel. Opened in 2009, the shop also works closely with the nearby Brooklyn Academy of Music (BAM). It's open until 22.00 daily.
greenlightbookstore.com

04 Strand, Union Square: Dating back to 1927, Strand's inventory permanently overflows onto the pavement (you could spend hours browsing the $1 outdoor racks). But inside is well worth a peek: four levels cover every subject imaginable, from entire bookcases devoted to dog breeding to rare first editions.
strandbooks.com

Accessories and specialist retailers
Devil in the detail

①

CO Bigelow, West Village
Favourite pharmacy

Founded in 1838, CO Bigelow (originally known as The Village Apothecary) is the oldest institution of its kind in the US. This venerable spot has its own line of sundries available, some dating far into its history. Its wooden shelves are stocked with anything you could possibly need or want in terms of toiletries.

That said, even if you're not in need of any essentials it's still worth a visit just to parade around a shop that has catered to the likes of Thomas Edison, Samuel Clemens and Eleanor Roosevelt.
414 Avenue of the Americas, NY 10011
+ 1 212 533 2700
bigelowchemists.com

I've packed plenty into this city break

②

Adore Floral, Noho
Flower power

Husband-and-wife team Jack Wu and Chiyomi Uchino founded Adore Floral in 2005, wanting to add a modern and diverse flower shop to Noho. Wooden floors and tables provide a natural backdrop to vases scattered throughout the shop, filled with greenery spanning from the unusual to the ordinary. With a rather ample assortment of flowers, the knowledgeable staff provide a welcome counsel if needed. If you want to send flowers as a thank you, allow them to work their magic to arrange and wrap to perfection.
357 Lafayette Street, NY 10012
+ 1 212 925 8182
adorenyc.com

③

The Meadow, West Village
Gifting genius

While some might consider a shop like The Meadow indulgent, the Portland-based owner of this speciality store, Mark Bitterman, thinks of it as a celebration of "classical pleasures": namely salt, chocolate and flowers. Shelves are lined on one side with fine chocolate bars and on the other an array of jars featuring everything from Icelandic black salt to Italian truffle salt. Fresh flowers keep a romantic atmosphere throughout the shop, where you can also find a range of spices, bitters and barware.
523 Hudson Street, NY 10014
+ 1 212 645 4633
atthemeadow.com

4

Moscot, Lower East Side
Everything eyewear

Century-old family-owned eyewear company Moscot is a New York institution. Having spent 77 years at the same storefront on the corner of Delancey and Orchard streets, its iconic yellow and black signage is a seemingly immutable part of the LES landscape. Sadly it was forced to move when the building was recently sold but fortunately not too far.

The new space aims to capture much of the essence of the old shop, including original furniture such as a 1920s countertop and 1940s drawers. Expect to find an extensive range of timeless eyewear and sunglasses, from its Moscot Originals collection to more contemporary adaptations.
108 Orchard Street, NY 10002
+ 1 212 477 3796
moscot.com

New York's given my specs appeal a real boost

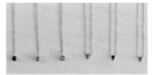

⑤ Mociun, Williamsburg
Artist's sensibility

With a background in textile design, Caitlin Mociun opened her shop in 2012. Craft and fine art play a central role at the core of this design space. What started as a small collection of women's garments has now evolved into a larger retail venture featuring accessories, home goods and beauty products. The shop is located near Williamsburg's waterfront and Mociun's careful eye has meant it is filled with worthy items: look out for woven baskets from Doug Johnston and ceramics by Eric Bonnin.
224 Wythe Avenue, NY 11249
+1 718 387 3731
mociun.com

⑥ Leffot, West Village
Footwear champion

Leffot's motto of *nunquam jactate* (never boast) seems particularly appropriate given the location of this excellent shoe shop: the quietly understated and subtly affluent West Village. Leffot's founder Steven Taffel (who previously spent 10 years with Prada) opened the space in 2008 with the aim of filling a gap in the market for high-quality men's shoes.

True to the New York aesthetic, Leffot's interior is minimally furnished with black wallpaper, big tables and bare floors. But that doesn't mean that it isn't well stacked with gems from around the world. The first-class range of brogues and boots on offer has been selected from some of the world's best brands, among them the likes of Church's, Alden, Saint Crispin's and Edward Green. Step inside.
10 Christopher Street, NY 10014
+1 212 989 4577
leffot.com

⑦ Acorn, Boerum Hill
Play time

Located in Boerum Hill, Acorn is a neighbourhood toy shop that has been serving a design-savvy clientele since 2004. Run by Diane Crespo and Karin Schaefer, the focus is squarely on timeless goods from wooden toys to clothing. "When we started there were hardly any handcrafted toy shops in New York," says co-owner Schaefer, who adds that most of the items are for children up to the age of six, although there are some toys designed for the six-to-12 age range.
323 Atlantic Avenue, NY 11201
+1 718 522 3760
acorntoyshop.com

Perfect picks

01 Playforever cars by Julian Meagher
02 Pillows from Coral and Tusk
03 Cases and shelves by Sinclair Smith & Co
04 Wooden toys by David Weeks
05 Clothing by Oeuf

⑧
NikeLab, Soho
Sneaker sensation

NikeLab makes sense in a city like New York, where walking miles in a single day is routine. This outlet of the Portland-based sportswear brand combines practicality with style and offers collaborations with the likes of Brazilian designer Pedro Lourenço, Britain's Mo'Wax or Berlin-based Johanna F Schneider to give its collections a kick. NikeLab's All Conditions Gear encompasses city sportswear designed for greater adaptability, movement and comfort – whether on gym floors or concrete-jungle streets.
21 Mercer Street, NY 10013
+1 212 226 5433
nike.com

Record shops
Sound choice

Beards and vinyl? They have never gone out of style

①
Turntable Lab, East Village
Vinyl pushers

This neighbourly record shop is the perfect place to stock up on new music while you're in town. DJ equipment is prominent but Turntable Lab also boasts a keen selection of new and used vinyl, from house and electronic to jazz and hip-hop. The clean, contemporary space is neatly designed with well-organised crates and shelves so you won't have to do too much rummaging. Staff are refreshingly welcoming to novices and aficionados alike and are more than happy to help you find what you're looking for.
120 East 7th Street, NY 10009
+1 212 677 0675
turntablelab.com

Three more

01 Black Gold Records,
Brooklyn:
Vintage records across
a variety of genres plus
coffee and antiques.
blackgoldbrooklyn.com

02 Good Records NYC,
East Village:
New and used vinyl,
and live performances.
goodrecordsnyc.com

03 Other Music,
Greenwich Village:
The focus is on indie,
rare vinyls and CDs.
othermusic.com

Street markets
Outdoor shopping

Fort Greene Flea, Brooklyn
City institution

Every Saturday from April to
November, the 3,700 sq m
schoolyard at Bishop Loughlin
Memorial High School in Brooklyn
is transformed into a market for
vintage finds, handmade crafts
and the best of local street-food
stalls. Among the 150 vendors are
artisan leather-goods makers such
as Flux Productions, book-seller
Greenlight, vintage clothing retailer
Bogart & Moore and the state-
grown wood worked by artisans
at NYCitySlab.

Of course, perusing the booths
will work up an appetite; luckily
there are vegetable or pork
dumplings from The Good Fork,
lobster rolls from Red Hook
Lobster Pound or Brooklyn
sodas for a refresher. Though
Brooklyn Flea can also be found
in Williamsburg, the original
location in Fort Greene boasts
the best (and least overrun)
atmosphere.
*176 Lafayette Avenue, NY 11238
brooklynflea.com*

Three more

01 Chelsea Market:
A food hall, shopping
mall and office building
all under one roof.
chelseamarket.com

02 Hester Street Fair, Lower
East Side:
A spring/summer street
fair offering food, jewellery,
clothing and crafts.
hesterstreetfair.com

03 Sugar Hill Market, Harlem:
A Sunday market
showcasing local
designers and artisans.
*sugarhillmarketnyc.
blogspot.com*

Things we'd buy
—— Perfect presents

You wouldn't want to leave New York without at least something for your nearest and dearest (not to mention yourself). Obviously there are some items we would love to have but they just aren't that practical for fitting in a suitcase: a Shinola bike, for example, or a mid-century piece of Brazilian furniture from Espasso, perhaps. Or even an axe from Best Made Company but you might struggle to get that one past security, so we've recommend one of its blankets instead.

We've sorted through the thousands of shops – sidestepping the tourist tack – to give you a selection of what we'd take away with us, from bourbon to shorts via a cookbook. Then there's the baseball cap and cold-brew coffee as well. It would be rude not to.

01 Dean & Deluca spice rub gift set and chocolate espresso beans *deandeluca.com*
02 Coin pouches by Shinola *shinola.com*
03 CO Bigelow shaving cream *bigelowchemists.com*
04 *Linda Gerard: Fabulous Selections* vinyl from Ace Hotel *shop.acehotel.com*
05 Bourbon from Widow Jane *widowjane.com*
06 Women's Elsa Peretti bean pendant by Tiffany & Co *tiffany.com*
07 DMFD tableware by Daniel Michalik *danielmichalik.com*
08 Mighty Tree spinning top by Karl Zahn *karlzahn.com*
09 Chocolates by Mast Brothers Chocolate Makers *mastbrothers.com*

10 Faribault Woollen Mill Co scarf *faribaultmill.com*
11 Grady's Cold Brew Iced Coffee Concentrate *gradyscoldbrew.com*
12 New York Fly TWA print from Moma *momastore.org*
13 Shorts by Saturdays *saturdaysnyc.com*
14 Lumberlander Camp Blanket by Best Made Company *bestmade.com*
15 Scented candle from Odin New York *odinnewyork.com*
16 Moisturiser by CO Bigelow *bigelowchemists.com*
17 *The Essential New York Times Cookbook* by Amanda Hesser *nytimes.com*

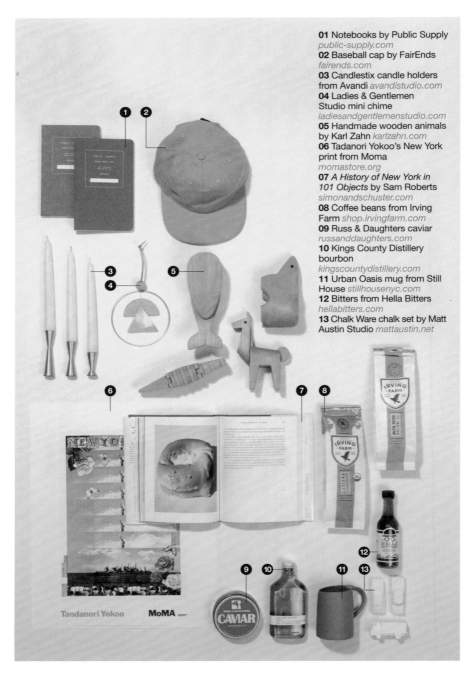

01 Notebooks by Public Supply
public-supply.com
02 Baseball cap by FairEnds
fairends.com
03 Candlestix candle holders
from Avandi *avandistudio.com*
04 Ladies & Gentlemen
Studio mini chime
ladiesandgentlemenstudio.com
05 Handmade wooden animals
by Karl Zahn *karlzahn.com*
06 Tadanori Yokoo's New York
print from Moma
momastore.org
07 *A History of New York in
101 Objects* by Sam Roberts
simonandschuster.com
08 Coffee beans from Irving
Farm *shop.irvingfarm.com*
09 Russ & Daughters caviar
russanddaughters.com
10 Kings County Distillery
bourbon
kingscountydistillery.com
11 Urban Oasis mug from Still
House *stillhousenyc.com*
12 Bitters from Hella Bitters
hellabitters.com
13 Chalk Ware chalk set by Matt
Austin Studio *mattaustin.net*

12 essays
—— Beyond the
city limits

*Plenty to
keep a
bird brain
engaged*

ESSAY 01

City of the imagination
New York's storied history

———

From Lou Reed's decadent street poetry to Woody Allen's silver-screen love letters, New York has inspired some of the greatest works of music, film and literature. But it remains a city that demands to be experienced first-hand.

*by Aisha Speirs,
Monocle*

It's an intimidating thing to start an essay on a city that thousands have written novels, films and songs about. New York is a place that, for one reason or another, gets people excited. You can't watch *Goodfellas* or the opening scene of *Manhattan*, listen to anyone from Duke Ellington to Lou Reed nor read Tom Wolfe, Paul Auster or even Henry James without romanticising the metropolis yourself. You don't even have to step foot in the place: New York does enough to make its streets, people and attitude a globally understood brand. It's assumed that everyone knows what New York stands for.

As Wolfe wrote in the *Bonfire of the Vanities*, "One belongs to New York instantly, one belongs to it as much in five minutes as in five years." There are few cities in the world that can claim that.

Your New York may be Jerry Seinfeld's or Jay Z's; it could be Jay Gatsby's or Esther Greenwood's. You may not be a native New Yorker but it's unlikely you'll arrive in the city without some idea of what you want it to be for you.

New York is a place of noise, talent and energy. Even time – that most unalterable of concepts – gets bent. A "New York minute" is said to be faster than any 60 seconds you or I think we know. It's a city where people speak frankly. It's where the best and the brightest of not only the US but the world flock to conquer their dreams. We're told of New York that if you can make it there you can make it anywhere. It's not a place that just embodies the American Dream: it's the Puerto Rican, Nigerian, Russian and Chinese dream. It's the dream of the millions of immigrants that made it and continue to feed it. It's New York that we associate with leading campaigns for civil, gay and women's rights. It's in New York that we believe we can achieve something as long as we're prepared to give everything. This brand of New York seems timeless yet it's a city much younger than London, Paris and Rome – all capitals of countries (New York City isn't even the capital of its own state) that have weathered more but often seem to have less. New York appears to be home to many cultures and languages yet it remains one of America's most segregated cities. We've seen New York serve as the centre of financial greed and dysfunction but businesses still seek its zip codes for their headquarters. Its public transport is old,

"There are few sights more magical than the deep orange-yellow light cast along these New York streets as the sun sets"

its roads are pot-holed and its airports are inefficient yet it continues to attract millions of visitors each year.

How does New York do it? Is there something in its geography? A city of five boroughs, all but one on islands, it grew as one of America's most important ports. Now Manhattan's long east-west streets and north-south avenues form vistas that unblock the island's predominantly vertical development. During winter the harsh, cold wind that barrels between the Hudson and East rivers feels like it could freeze your nose off; but during long summer evenings there are few sights more magical than the deep orange-yellow light cast along these streets as the sun sets.

Manhattan's avenues can be walked all the way from the Financial District – with its views of the Statue of Liberty and neighbouring New Jersey – through colourful Chinatown, gentrified Soho and frenetic Midtown up to the unchanging Upper East Side and reinvented Harlem.

Brooklyn is home to everything from dive bars to Russian beachside nightclubs; Staten Island has nature reserves and a historic Italian population; the Bronx has a 500-hectare park around an 18th-century country house; and riding the 7 train in Queens takes you through Turkish, Indian, Irish and Taiwanese neighbourhoods and all the cuisines that are found in them.

There is no better city in which to feel the full four seasons of the year than New York. During summer, trips to Long Island's beaches and harbours make for easy weekend breaks. Upstate farms and orchards are perfect backdrops for the changing colours of autumn and during winter, the city's bars and restaurants offer shelter from the regular snowfall and sub-zero temperatures outside. The best time of year by far is during the first days of spring: cafés put out their outdoor seating, joggers seem to run more lightly and New York's parks, pavements, rooftops and terraces come alive for the beginning of a good six months of outdoor urban living.

I don't quite know what it is that makes New York tick but I do know that despite its many flaws, it's not hard to write a love letter to the place. It's a city where I no longer live nor yearn to return to but it will always be somewhere that means more to me (and many others) than simply a point on the map. No matter how much there is to read, watch or hear about New York, it's a city that will always have the final word. — (M)

ABOUT THE WRITER: Aisha Speirs moved to New York from London in early 2008. She worked at *Surface Magazine* before joining MONOCLE in late 2009. She lived in Brooklyn, Chinatown, Nolita and the West Village before moving to Hong Kong in 2013 to become bureau chief. She misses Manhattan dive bars.

A Bronx tale
Overlooked corners

Once bucolic retreats and then pariahs of New York, the Bronx and Staten Island have complicated histories in common. It's fitting, then, that the two boroughs are experiencing a renaissance together.

by Jordan Hruska, author, journalist and critic

Visitors to New York often neglect a trip to the outer boroughs of the Bronx and Staten Island due to their respective reputations as a place of high crime and a remote bedroom community. But as crime drops to historic lows and the city's population increases, these boroughs are welcoming new residents and visitors by illuminating their histories and becoming cultural destinations in their own right.

Their arms weren't always open. Despite both being incorporated into New York in 1898, the Bronx and Staten Island seemed further from their municipal seat than ever before towards the end of the 20th century. In the 1970s the Bronx was a veritable warzone of arson fires and drug activity that scarred the urban landscape with abandoned buildings and homeless residents.

Infamous news footage of then presidential candidate Ronald Reagan on the 1980 campaign trail in the South Bronx shows him walking through urban rubble and arguing with local residents who plea for help. The borough has come a long way since then but as recently as 2010 the US Census reported that South Bronx was the poorest district in America – an anomaly within a city then cited as being home to the world's largest concentration of billionaires.

When it comes to municipal and state politics, Staten Island has traditionally been more conservative than the rest of liberal New York. Often the black sheep of political discussions, this largely working-class borough felt so divorced from city politics that it voted in 1993 to secede,

"The Bronx and Staten Island's most charming qualities shine through because they're located on the city's edges"

Things to see in the Bronx
—
01 Wave Hill
Estate-turned-art gallery with magnificent gardens.
02 John Muir Trail at Van Cortlandt Park
Fertile trail in one of the city's most underrated parks.
03 Gino's Pastry Shop
For the canolis.

a referendum reversed by the New York State Assembly. But New York is full of residents who find pride in their independence.

The Bronx and Staten Island's most charming qualities shine through because they're located on the edges, allowing visitors to discover their uniquely built and natural environments outside the numbing bustle of Manhattan.

The Bronx was largely developed in the late 19th century as an escape from the city. Today you can still catch your breath in the borough's many parks or lose your breath rooting for the Yankees (affectionately dubbed the "Bronx Bombers") at Yankee Stadium.

Hemmed in by the winding Harlem River to the south, the Hudson River to the west and the Long Island Sound to the east, the Bronx thrusts northward from Manhattan towards the granite ridges of New York state's Hudson Valley. Dramatic hills rise and fall within the borough, which is stitched through the centre by the wide boulevard of The Grand Concourse, constructed in 1909 in the vein of Paris's Champs-Élysées. This concourse is a trove of art deco architecture, the largest collection in the US. By bike you can ride the length of the avenue and marvel at all the brushed aluminium, glass bricks and geometrically crenellated detail. Of note is the so-called Fish Building, designed by Horace Ginsbern. It features a swirling, undersea-inspired mosaic on its street-level façade in addition to a red, green and gold terrazzo lobby floor and soaring lobby murals.

Just like the Bronx, Staten Island was known as a bucolic escape for the city's 19th-century residents who built waterfront homes here. Despite the borough's rapid development, preservationists have fought hard to maintain the island's historic buildings and natural shoreline, much of which you can see on the approach from the ferry. One such industrialist purchased a holiday home here in 1844 into which his granddaughter Alice Austen moved shortly thereafter. After receiving a camera for a gift, Austen quietly became a prolific street photographer, a rarity for women at the time. Her work is collected in this 1690s home, now preserved by the city as The Alice Austen House, which also shows rotating exhibitions of contemporary photography and boasts sweeping views of New York Harbor from its lawn.

Locals informally divide Staten Island between the North Shore facing Manhattan and Brooklyn and the South Shore, which is closer in proximity and feel to the state of New Jersey. Neighbourhoods in the south feature some of the best 24-hour diners in New York, which also function as ad-hoc community centres for Staten Islanders. Adventurous day-trippers can visit the hamlet of Rossville on the South Shore to take in the Ruins of Rossville, an inlet featuring half-submerged mid-century boats, collapsed piers and other once-seafaring rusted detritus.

But despite this decaying spectacle, Staten Island is rising ever taller. By 2017 the North Shore is scheduled to feature the New York Wheel, which developers boast will be the world's tallest observation wheel and a major landmark to rival the Statue of Liberty within the theatre of New York Harbor. Not to be outdone, the Bronx is set to open its own superlative site not long after. Developers will renovate the massive beaux arts Kingsbridge Armory into the world's largest indoor ice centre featuring nine recreational rinks. Further proof that these once outer boroughs are now definitely in. — (M)

ABOUT THE WRITER: Jordan Hruska is a New York-based art historian, critic and journalist covering design, architecture and travel. He is the co-author of 2011 book *The Library of Philip Johnson: Selections from the Glass House*.

ESSAY 03

The subway sects
Transport battle lines

———

How you choose to get about in New York not only defines your experience of the city but also says a lot about your personality. For some, the iconic subterranean train system is truly the only way to travel.

by Tristan McAllister, Monocle

I have a friend who loves to push my transport buttons. He is convinced that riding New York's subways is a privilege. He stops at nothing to be sure we never use a car service or flag a taxi while crossing town. I, on the other hand, like things easy. Sure, I love public transport but I also like getting to where I am going with relative ease, peace and the option of rolling down the window.

What we agree on is that there is some beauty in New York's transport system. For instance, the late Massimo Vignelli developed a brand book for the system in the 1970s. The famed designer also sketched a map that, while lauded by designers, the public was critical of, leading it to be reworked in 1979. "Vignelli's design was superior because people read schematics more easily than squiggly lines," says my friend, criticising the existing one. I agree but I can't help wonder if a New York newcomer might appreciate the geographic features of the map as it is.

Based loosely on Vignelli's design, the current map is proudly displayed on the system's tile walls from the Bronx to Lower Manhattan. The illustration of colour-coded lines and numbers is a nice souvenir if you can snag a copy from the brochure rack tucked into MTA (Metropolitan Transportation Authority) information kiosks. But the creative promise of a Vignelli map can seem a distant notion while in the bowels of the MTA.

To help daunted holidaymakers cope, I'd tell them to remember that this city is not about grand welcoming gestures or trivial pleasantries. My friend would tell them it's all about embracing things like the intimate moments you might spend with one of five million or more strangers onboard the uptown-bound F train.

He'd say that for a few stops you may catch someone's eye, or they yours. He'd extol the virtues of the chat a fellow rider might start with you, commenting on the book you're reading, or simply asking you if you need directions. Compare this to the quiet experience you'll find on a train in Tokyo or London and you're already well on your way to feeling engaged. Once you've disembarked you come to understand that you could possibly have had a whole week's worth of peculiar interactions all in one ride. And then you realise that your visit to New York is punctuated by these moments that could only happen here. Which brings both of us to a point that may even defeat my preference for surface transport.

> *"Riding the subway is all about embracing things like the intimate moments you might spend with one of five million or more strangers onboard the uptown-bound F train"*

There are certain times of day when it's impossible to flag a taxi. I've stood on the street outside our New York bureau and lobbed my hand into the air, only to be left disappointed and late for a meeting or dinner date. When a cab is flagged down, the driver will typically ask you where you're headed. If you're not headed in his or her direction they'll just speed off.

Beyond that, when a cab is actually willing to pick you up, you still need to be very aware of the ground game going on around you. Are you "upstream" or "downstream"? By that I mean, is there someone a block up the street from you hailing a cab? If there is then you are "downstream", which means all the cabs will be taken before they get to you and you're better off in the subway. It's at these particular moments my friend likes to remind me that the subway isn't that crowded and it runs all day.

So my friend makes some good points. And for the record, I usually end up riding underground anyway. The key here is mixing it up and embracing all the unexpected things that happen along the way. Let this happen and the journey could prove rewarding. Who knows? If you stare long enough at your admirer on the subway you may end up leaving the city with more than a goofy T-shirt. — (M)

ABOUT THE WRITER: Tristan McAllister is MONOCLE's transport editor. When he first moved to New York from Portland he had to learn how to navigate through trial and error. To this day he's still partial to his Bianchi and the great bike paths through the city.

Key subway stations

01 Jay Street-MetroTech
Transfer station of choice for many a commuter.
02 Broadway-Lafayette Street
You can connect with the B, D, M, 4 and 6 from here.
03 Times Square – 42nd Street
Brings you into the hubbub of Midtown.

ESSAY 04

Tasting the apple
The city's signature dishes

New York's ever-evolving restaurant scene of fusion foods and craft beers is exhilarating. But round-the-block queues mean many are instead looking towards the simple delis and dishes adored by the city's elders.

*by Julia Sherman,
writer and photographer*

As a food writer and photographer obsessed with all things edible, I treat every meal as if it were my last. And in my food-obsessed city I am certainly not alone; planning dinner in New York is a contest of wills. Beleaguered by the pursuit of the most fashionable restaurants, some of us are now finding comfort in the traditional foods that we grew up taking for granted. Jewish food, once unique to the deli, has suddenly been thrown into relief. Entirely unconcerned with the dizzying culinary landscape, these tried and true establishments of the Upper West and Lower East sides have done the impossible: maintained their bricks-and-mortar establishments with original decor since the turn of the 20th century. Their recipes have refused to react to trends and, as a result, those hearty postwar immigrant Jews have bequeathed to us, their far more fickle descendants, the schmaltz-laden cuisine of our ancestors.

When I was planning a lunch with a formidable culinary magazine editor, she generously gave me a choice of three restaurants: Dimes, the Lower East Side café; La Grenouille, the glamorous Midtown French institution for ladies who lunch for a living; and, last but not least, Barney Greengrass, the charmingly crusty, old-world Jewish deli on the Upper West Side. I was tickled to see the chichi La Grenouille in a line-up with Barney Greengrass, with its over-sized laminated menu of whitefish salad, chopped chicken liver and

Sherman's top Jewish-inspired NY dishes

01 Gefilte fish
Light fish ball served with horseradish.
02 Chopped chicken liver
A Passover staple in my grandmother's house.
03 Whitefish salad
Smoked fish and mayo spread on a bagel.

"The first generation of American Jews guarded traditions of their cuisine in a city always on the hunt for the next big thing" matzo balls. These homely but tasty dishes, always served with a "garnish" of iceberg lettuce, once belonged to the Sams, the Pearls, the Roses and the Mortimers of the city: the first generation of American Jews who jealously guarded the traditions of their cuisine in a city always on the hunt for the next big thing.

My late grandpa Sam was himself like a bagel with lox and a schmear of cream cheese: something to be enjoyed in its purest, most reliably static form. No matter the occasion or the destination, "Jewish food" was the only food I remember him openly agreeing to and Barney Greengrass was his place of choice. He grew up in Borough Park, Brooklyn, with five sisters and a mother who spoke only Yiddish. He began his adult life as a factory assembly-line worker, only to become the owner of a mini property empire. He was not alone in this trajectory but part of a whole generation of immigrant Jews who, with little formal education and not a penny to their names, managed to scoot their way from the Lower East Side up to Park Avenue in no time.

Despite a drastic uptick in tax bracket and a far more desirable postcode, grandpa Sam's palate was unchanged. It was in the comfort of these old-world establishments that my far more fashionable grandmother would let him wear his old grey polyester trousers, oversized plastic glasses and knock-off gold Rolex, far too big for his wrist and dangling loose like a bracelet. (My father eventually gave him a real one but it never saw the light of day; he was happy with the fake he already had.)

New Yorkers two generations later romanticise the city of yesteryear in one breath and fawn over the newest hot spot in the next. Over contemporary Brooklyn nibbles and craft cocktails we compete for whose rose-coloured memories are most vivid, trying to prove that within us remains a bygone, authentic Big Apple.

So it should come as no surprise that Jewish delis serving a cuisine that has managed to buck all trends should be en vogue. Nor that Russ & Daughters would open a café and be the talk of the town; nor that wholesale Acme Smoked Fish in Brooklyn would have lines outside its warehouse door during its brief Friday retail hours. There are few things in New York that seem indestructible but if Barney Greengrass, "The Sturgeon King", was to close it would cause a riot.

It is a dubious privilege to claim proprietary nostalgia for the Williamsburg of the early 2000s, or for Soho before Chanel laid its roots in the area. Given the lightning speed with which businesses open and close in this town, these reflections on the past decade can seem profound. But I have to laugh on behalf of my elders, who wouldn't move back to Brooklyn for all the money in the world.

I happily wait in line at Acme Smoked Fish, I trek to the ends of the Earth (Amsterdam and 87th Street) for that legendary sturgeon and I reassure my nana that yes indeed, I would love for her to order a log of fresh gefilte fish from Fischer Bros & Leslie to be delivered to my house in Brooklyn. She takes great pleasure in knowing that I am spreading the gospel and sharing quality produce with my friends, gentile and Jewish alike. Trying to convince the uninitiated, I hear my nana's words coming out of my mouth verbatim: "Trust me, this is not the gelatinous Manischewitz stuff from a jar. This fish is freshly made at Fischer Brothers; it's the best fish money can buy."

Seriously, don't knock it till you try it. Gefilte fish is the next big thing. — (M)

ABOUT THE WRITER: Julia Sherman is the editor, photographer and writer behind Salad for President, an ongoing project about food, art and everyday obsessions. She also created the first ever Moma PS1 rooftop salad garden.

ESSAY 05

Insider knowledge
Rolling out the welcome mat

—

A concierge's job is far more than providing bus times and subway maps. It's about inviting the customer into your world and making them feel like a true New Yorker.

*by Dwight Owsley,
hotel concierge*

I first moved to New York in 1980. I had studied opera back in my native Texas and moved to the Big Apple to continue my studies and hopefully become a singer. When I found out the price of voice lessons that initial idea quickly went out the window and I had to find a *real* job – so I came to The Carlyle. Peter Jay Sharp, the owner of the hotel at the time who died in 1992, had a particular vision of how a concierge should be. He was a serious New Yorker and his foundation helped a lot of people; you can still see his name on buildings dotted around town.

Peter liked his concierges to have character. Anyone can tell you what time the next bus leaves but not everyone can advise on how the opera season is shaping up and which play would be appropriate for your grandmother. He hired opinionated people to be concierges. I remember he took on a French and German linguist and then he hired me because of my love for theatre and opera.

We all came with our own idiosyncrasies that were honed and refined at The Carlyle to benefit guests.

Crime was higher back in the 1980s and the city has changed for the better since then. New Yorkers have become worldlier and more cosmopolitan. The urban landscape has changed too: where Lincoln Center is now – co-founded by Sharp – was a Latino neighbourhood. I used to work with people who lived there when it had a gang problem. Under President Eisenhower the housing estates – what we call "the projects" – were torn down and Lincoln Center filled the void, creating a cultural centre.

My job has changed a lot over the years, too. When I started, the hotel world was more genteel. "Popular" luxury hadn't yet been introduced; customers arrived by limousine. I was never asked to produce a tourist map or look up train timetables for that matter, except using the old *Thomas Cook European Timetable*, a venerable tome first published in 1873.

With the rise of the internet, we were worried that people weren't going to need concierges, especially in technologically advanced cities such as New York. But the truth is that people would still rather interact with a human being; this applies even to the younger generation. Planning with the help of a concierge is far more insightful than booking something last minute over the internet.

When you go online to see the Broadway listings, often you find yourself limited to what can fit on the page. Visitors want to talk to someone who has had interaction with other people who have seen the show to have an idea of what it's like. With new guests, the trick is to gain insight into their personalities and figure out what makes them tick.

"When I first started at The Carlyle as a concierge the hotel world was far more genteel. 'Popular' luxury hadn't yet been introduced; customers always arrived by limousine"

I've seen it all at The Carlyle: I've enjoyed speaking with Princess Diana and the King of Sweden. I remember when Elizabeth Taylor was staying here during her run on Broadway in *The Little Foxes*. When she would call down for something her voice would change depending on whoever was in the room; she was such an accomplished actress. And I remember when Jessye Norman, the opera singer, was playing Delilah in *Samson and Delilah* at Carnegie Hall and had just returned to the hotel after performing. She was standing at the door of the Café Carlyle where cabaret musician Bobby Short was playing. He gazed around the room, finally resting his gaze on Jessye, who had just pushed the door open a little. "Jessye, I'm singing now. Would you care to join me?" he asked. Her response was to break into song: "I don't know but I shall try!"

I've been here for more than 30 years so I'm like part of the family. I'm now helping the grandchildren of people I served when I first arrived. I've grown wiser but I've also realised that everything can't go right all of the time. — (M)

ABOUT THE WRITER: Dwight Owsley has been a concierge at The Carlyle hotel in New York since 1981. He lives a short walk away on the Upper East Side. He taught himself opera and took private lessons to fuel his passion; his all-time favourites are *Carmen* and *La Traviata*.

Star-studded stays
——
01 Waldorf Astoria, Midtown
Grace Kelly and Prince Rainier
of Monaco, 1956.
02 The Carlyle,
Upper East Side
The Duke and Duchess
of Cambridge, 2014.
03 The Warwick, Midtown
The Beatles, 1966.

The daily grind
Returning coffee capital

———

New York's craft-coffee revolution has spread across its five boroughs, evoking a time when the city's coffeehouses sat at the centre of its trade expansion.

by Chad Freilino, restaurant consultant

In New York the cornershop or "deli" is an institution. You can get everything there: a cream-cheese bagel, fresh flowers or a lottery ticket. For most New Yorkers this is where the day starts, with a breakfast on the go and a bracingly bad cup of coffee. It's a distinctly East Coast experience, complete with an iconic blue-and-white paper cup proudly boasting the phrase "we are happy to serve you" (*see the Design and architecture section on page 109*). But in spite of this tradition, or perhaps because of it, coffee in New York is getting better and makers from the fast-growing speciality coffee industry are supplanting the kitsch cups of yesteryear.

The shops at the forefront of New York's contemporary coffee boom focus intensely on origin and preparation. They do so within spaces designed to feel like coffee cathedrals – a far cry from those aforementioned corner delis. Good coffee has infiltrated even the most far-flung neighbourhoods (I'm looking at you, Bushwick). It has spawned a revolution in craft-level products from bakery to brewing devices and ignited a new passion for design as part of the coffee experience. In short: New York is getting its coffee credentials back.

When, in 1773, the American colonists dumped a hoard of tea – that most English of beverages – into Boston's harbour during a tax dispute with the crown, they turned to the Dutch and their coffee for a caffeine fix. Since then coffee has been the drink of choice for Americans and for a long time New York was the centre of the industry. Merchants offloaded green, unroasted coffee at docks on the Hudson and East rivers. The beans were roasted in

Favourite roasters
———
01 Irving Farm
Perfect example of a true NY coffee roaster.
02 Stumptown
One of the most beautiful examples in New York.
03 Pulley Collective
For aspiring roasters who need a place to turn their beans brown.

"When, in 1773, the American colonists dumped a hoard of tea into Boston's harbour, they turned to the Dutch and their coffee"

waterfront warehouses and from there provided the caffeine that fuelled the expansion of the US. Coffeehouses were the beating heart of New York's political and trade scenes. In the 1790s, the Tontine Coffee House on Wall Street was the birthplace of the New York Stock Exchange.

In the late 19th century, cities and infrastructure extended into the American west; the coffee industry migrated accordingly. New York ceased to be the centre of the US coffee universe but it still supported a truncated local industry. This continued until the 1970s and 1980s, when blue-collar-style manufacturing simply wasn't viable here. Local roasters and importers were squeezed out of valuable waterfront locations. For some time a small but dedicated coffee industry limped along in Manhattan. Fortunately, with white-collar businesses came expendable income and sophisticated tastes. Fast-evolving New Yorkers were ready for the next evolution in coffee.

Today, New York might once again be the coffee capital of the US. In cities such as Portland in Oregon and San Francisco you can't throw a rock without hitting a career barista but New York is big and dense and hides a surprising trove of exceptional coffee. There are around 40 roasters in New York serving some of the best beans on the planet. I'll bet my hat that's more than any other city in the world.

And it's not just in Manhattan. Brooklyn has developed its own coffee scene and is set to give the island of Manhattan a run for its money. You'll find many of American's big-name craft coffees setting up shop here. Brands such as Blue Bottle, Stumptown and Caffé Vita are all at loggerheads, competing to have the biggest and best roasting plants in neighbourhoods such as Bushwick and Red Hook. In revamped industrial warehouses you'll also find local brands such as Brooklyn Roasting and Pulley Collective adding voices to the chorus.

The dogfight for customer loyalty dictates that it's not enough to just have exceptional coffees and a local roasting plant. No, the enlightened coffee drinker demands a beautiful and inspiring space to sip his or her daily extraction. New York's fast-emerging speciality scene has no shortage of inspiring, if not incredibly overdone, spaces in which to get your fix.

This city has become a fascinating case study in coffee-shop design with an eclectic mix of old and new. Shops such as Caffé

Vita and Grumpy make do with less than 18.5 sq m on the Lower East Side, while Blue Bottle in Williamsburg is gargantuan by New York standards and includes an on-site roasting plant. At Toby's Estate in the Flatiron District you can buy a flat white alongside a rare book, an exquisite floral arrangement or a new spring wardrobe. What's clear is that New York's coffee shops have evolved a distinctly American sensibility.

For those of you not from the US, be prepared for American coffee. We prefer light roast espressos that are acidic and have a strong tendency toward academic flavours (think berries, vegetables and fruits) and single-origin coffees that are less about comfort and more about expanding our coffee horizons. You will hear a barista use the word *terroir* – and not at all ironically. So if trying new things is at all daunting to you, remember there's always that corner deli and its blue-and-white paper cups awaiting you. — (M)

ABOUT THE WRITER: Coffee programme director at a Manhattan-based restaurant group, Chad Freilino has worked in the industry for over a decade, honing his espresso chops in the craft scenes of Portland and Seattle. His top brew? The buttery smooth finish (and spicy chocolate notes) of beans from Chiapas, Mexico.

ESSAY 07
Keep your head up
Building skywards

___

The architectural triumphs of New York go beyond the Empire State Building: its history is told through the myriad styles visible down every avenue.

by Morris Adjmi, architect

Every visitor to New York comes away with a different version of the city. No wonder: New York has more stories than people and more variety than stories. If the narrative most visitors know is told through the city's well-known landmarks – the Chrysler and Empire State buildings, for instance – lesser-known buildings offer more unusual, layered tales. It's here that distinctive architecture and historic purpose speak to the New York not of tourism but of commerce, art and craft.

Wall Street is as much a concept as a place. And while it is indeed an interesting destination there is a far more intriguing icon of business: Cass Gilbert's Woolworth Building, which celebrated its centennial in 2013. The precedents it set – for more than 25 years the tallest building in the world, costing $13.5m, paid in cash – have been superseded. Its architectural distinction has not: the unusual blend of sacred and classical was a deliberate and very American association of spiritual enlightenment with monetary gain. It was no coincidence that a clergyman approvingly called it the "Cathedral of Commerce" (the nobility of the building's architecture was meant to imply the worthiness of its purpose). While the building's neo-gothic style is unlikely to make a comeback, terracotta is having something of a renaissance in the New York architectural scene: witness Renzo Piano's *New York Times* Building or the recladding of the Museum of Art and Design.

Head north into the neighbourhood known both as Soho – due to its location south of Houston Street – and the Cast Iron Historic District, for its distinctive and now landmarked architecture. Within this assemblage of late 19th-century buildings, 101 Spring Street stands out for a number of unusual, even unique features. The vault light system, most likely the only one of its kind in New York, brings daylight down through two basement levels. The cast-iron columns here, typically decorative overlays on interior supports, are part of the structure. That reliance on the strength of the metal anticipates steel skyscraper design. Even more significant is the building's function: acquired in 1968 by Donald Judd for his residence and studio it is considered the original realisation of his concept of "permanent installation", in which the placement of a work of art is as important as the work itself. Today it is home to the Judd Foundation, hosting tours and programmes on art, design and the cultural history of the district.

No Art Without Craft – Irene Tichenor's biography of the typographer and printer Theodore Low De Vinne – describes the

"A clergyman approvingly called Cass Gilbert's Woolworth Building the 'Cathedral of Commerce'"

transition across Houston Street into Noho (once considered part of Greenwich Village), where the 1886 De Vinne Press Building stands at Lafayette and 4th Street. Built to house De Vinne's printing company, the artistry of the building's architecture is revealed by the craft of its making. Almost entirely lacking in any extraneous "decoration", the two main brick façades have a straightforward industrial elegance; the structure overall has the substance and mass of a 19th-century printing press.

After the Civil War, the neighbourhood saw an influx of publishers, paper dealers, bookbinders, and periodicals of various kinds. While the buildings housing these establishments were larger and taller than De Vinne, none served as so powerful an anchor or have been so prudently cared for.

Journeying northeast uptown, the Ford Foundation building is both of and well ahead of its time. Designed with roots in the International Style by Kevin Roche and John Dinkeloo and completed in 1968, the building introduces a new vocabulary, materials and environmental controls. It foreshadows many of the principles – abandoned for decades – that today dominate architectural dialogue. The large garden courtyard gives nearly all occupants exterior views and natural light; the building's relationship with its surroundings binds the structure to the environment; and the then uncommon weathering steel of the envelope has become the signature of such artists as Richard Serra.

With all the dizzying variety of architectural styles, eras and functions, it can be easy not to look up enough. Keep looking to the very top and you'll see that New York is home to structures unique to this city, almost all identical and perched on rooftops: the water tanks. Though they have been around for some 150 years, nothing has changed: they are still made of wood; still assembled by hand on site, usually of cedar and erected in a single day; still round; and crowned with a conical cap. The skyline is marked by about 10,000 of them standing 25 metres tall. Some are surrounded by rooftop enclosures and occasionally whimsically designed but most are naked on an elevated base, anchored through beams to the building's supporting structure. With time and the elements the wood weathers, taking on a patina of New York grey.

Unlike so much of New York the tanks are generally plain and uncomplicated, without moving parts of multiple functions or adornment. They are elegant in their simplicity of form and function; the quintessential unifying element for all of the cities stories. — (M)

ESSAY 08

Pour relations
Non-miserly cocktails

Combining theatrical showmanship, full-strength drinks and effortless conversation, New York's free-pouring barmen define the city's pleasure experience.

by Robert Bound, Monocle

When your Jumbo's wheels squeal down JFK's tarmac that first time you'll wonder what all the fuss is about; it's just another landmark-free runway, after all. Then it all unfolds like a film, frame by frame, from the window of your Manhattan transfer. In the taxi you're spurred by the peaks of that silhouette of a skyline; that A-list Gothic etching, spiked like a cardiogram of a heart falling in love. Are you in love? You're falling into it; the best part. Now come with me and have a drink.

We'll seal the deal; you and me and NYC. I don't care if New York is the *home* of the free pour or not. Don't tell them but origins aren't Americans' strong suit. Origins

ABOUT THE WRITER: Morris Adjmi is the founder and principal of Morris Adjmi Architects, established in 1997 following a decade-long partnership with Italian architect Aldo Rossi. Adjmi has been an adjunct professor at Columbia University and sits on the board of Open House New York.

are in the old world and strain to like it as you might, you don't like the old world as much as you think you should because you can't speak the language. In New York though, with *that* accent? You'll clean up. Mind you, I'll keep my old-world manners in check or the barman'll add a dollar onto our drinks straight off the bat.

We'll sit at the bar. You want a booth? What, are you going to propose to me already? A banquette? *Spell* it. So we're sat on bar stools because we're here to see the free pour. It's an L-shaped bar and we're sitting on the ascender of that letter, not the descender because I'm funny about things like that and anyway, which way do we want the evening to go?

So we're about two thirds of the way down the back of the bar near the angle of the L, where we'll have the view of the place and we'll be served second quickest. You don't want a barman with an order pressurising him. Make a friend, allow the guy in the bow tie to mix yours with time on his side. First come, second served makes

"First come, second served makes for the better drink. And aids the illusion you didn't need one"

for the better drink. And aids the illusion you didn't *need* one.

Take a look at the bottles. I know. The night is young. We'll have dry martinis because they start the night and it's that sort of night and you've been on a plane and this will do something between ironing your creases and easing your forgetfulness that there ever were creases. And, later, help you see that creases are, in fact, as beautiful as snow-capped peaks from an airplane window, one of the stalagmites that make life aglimmer with wonderful fixes. Like the free pour.

Our friend will ask you how you'd like it because you haven't told him and you're not from round here (you're reading a travel guide, aren't you?). In New York, the presumption with martinis is, more or less, that they're made with vodka. It's not intolerable to have to say "gin" and then whichever make or shape of bottle you prefer. Once that's done, stick with a twist or an olive and settle in to watch the show.

The free pour makes New York the best place in the world to drink a cocktail. Cocktails. You shouldn't be in a place that calls a barman a "mixologist" because you'd be pushed into places like that by a

New York drinking dens
—
01 Von, Noho
Long bar, strong drinks, grown-up, classic.
02 The Shanty, Williamsburg
Attached to its own distillery so it shouldn't run out.
03 Baby Grand, Little Italy
Tiny karaoke den made for fun and games.

different sort of guidebook. But you will see a certain flair, some pride, some knowledge, a craft being practised with expertise. What do you do for a living? Bar staff do *this* and you're watching the free pour. No half measures, no measures at all, no messing with steel scales, no eyeing-up of the line of the metric or miserly lab-coated carefulness. Instead, the ice to cool the metal – thrown in, thrown out – the arc of clear liquid as it hits its mark in the well of the shaker, the shake, the stir, the wham-bam-thank-you-very-much-indeed, sir/ma'am of a pure, concise process. All done in the name of making a $10 thing worth more than that $10. You could call it love. Another? You could call it working for a tip.

You're in tipping country here, even at the bar; especially at the bar. The tip is the other great civility of the free pour: not only the show of skill that it's a joy to behold and the acknowledgement that we're all adults here but the fact that you get what you pay for. You scratch my back and I'll promise to forget the arithmetic. Then it's up to you. Do you feel better, like you own a little bit of New York? We've seen some daylight shine in upon magic. And we're out into the night. — (M)

ABOUT THE WRITER: Robert Bound is MONOCLE's Culture editor. He also hosts the *Culture* show on Monocle 24 radio station; tune in every Monday at 19.00 UK time, 14.00 EST.

ESSAY 09
Play to the calorie
Eat, eat, crave, repeat

———

From the waistline-wrecking leviathan of the doughnut burger to the panacea of trendy kale, New York provides a spectrum-wide taste sensation 24 hours a day. And the choice just keeps on growing.

*by Joel Todd,
Winkreative*

New York is notoriously a place of extremes: rich and poor, hot and cold, uptown and downtown. This is also evident in the city's food culture, an epicurean playground that caters to every indulgence and whim. Temptation lies around every corner; you can happily eat and drink yourself silly one day and absolve yourself of sin the next.

Of course, you can find some of the best cooking in the world in New York and the restaurant scene here – and it is definitely a "scene" – is thriving. But the city is also famed for less refined, more immediate gratifications: the hot dog, doughnuts, New York cheesecake, eggs Benedict, fried chicken, waffles and lobster rolls (the latter two albeit regional imports). Pizza may have originated in Italy but New York has made it its own. It would be very easy to come here for a long weekend and never see the inside of a museum, gallery or shop, simply rolling from one meal to the next.

New York is always on the lookout for the next incarnation of these familiar classics – and in this testing ground, more is more. Take the doughnut, for instance. Recent years have given us such variations as the "cronut", the maple-waffle doughnut and the doughnut burger. This latter salty-sweet hybrid – beef burger, bacon, cheese and a fried egg, all sandwiched between a glazed donut – might be too much for most to stomach but for others it's nirvana.

Weekend brunch – to New Yorkers what the Sunday roast is to Londoners – has evolved into a decadent, all-day affair that would make Henry VIII blush. Often this is haute comfort food; southern-influenced dishes such as confit duck with cheddar grits, biscuits and gravy or truffled mac'n'cheese.

If your waistband is beginning to strain after all this no-holds-barred gluttony, modern health shrines such as Organic Avenue and Juice Press offer salvation through salad, an experience that is equally as fetishised as the fat, starch and sugar-laden goods they aim to expunge. Kale is king here, cropping up in salad, soup and, most prominently, in juice. It's easy to see why there's now an organic cold-pressed juice bar on every corner: in a city short on time, small on kitchens and big on socialising, chugging one of these brightly coloured elixirs is an easy way for New Yorkers to keep themselves healthy. Or at least make them feel that way.

As a Brit in the US, it takes a while to come to terms with the fact that it is OK for you to have what you want, no matter how particular. You might think you sound totally neurotic and ridiculous ordering your "unblended acai bowl, hold the

"New York entices you with a bewildering range of food options; the problem isn't having what you want but knowing what you want"

agave, please" but others around you won't be paying attention. New Yorkers take their fitness very seriously.

This is the land of plenty but for the indecisive these experiences can be near panic-attack inducing. Walk into a salad bar and you'll be presented with an infinite combination of ingredients, from the type of tomato to the 20 different dressings on offer. But during a busy weekday lunchtime you'd better decide on your order in a New York minute; there's no time to dither here. New York frequently entices you with a bewildering range of food options and, as with so many things in life, often the problem isn't having what you want but *knowing* what you want.

You can eat and drink anything you desire in New York and at whatever time you choose. You want tacos delivered to your office mid-morning? No problem. You want to slurp ramen at midnight? Fine. Or how about an antioxidant amino-acid power juice injection after your 07.00 run? You got it. Popping across to the corner shop for a bottle of wine, however, is a little less easy. But that's enough subject matter for a whole other essay. — (M)

ABOUT THE WRITER: Born and raised in St Ives, Cornwall, Joel Todd has worked in design, branding and content for the last nine years. Now a senior account manager at Winkreative, he splits his time between New York and London. His favourite NY food? He's a big fan of the tacos from Tacombi.

ESSAY 10

In praise of progress
New York's evolution

———

The times, as they are inclined to do, have a-changed in this city over the past 100 years. Some bemoan lost grit and gentrification but those that do miss the point: a safer New York is a more open New York.

*by Ed Stocker,
Monocle*

Manhattan has a population density of some 69,000 people per square mile. OK, so this isn't quite on a par with Manila or Mumbai but it's a pretty sizeable figure nonetheless. Manhattan is by far the busiest county in the US and the relative calm of some of New York's outer boroughs says nothing of the energy, speed and sheer number of human bodies crammed onto the main island.

And yet despite all of this – or possibly because of it – New York manages to work. While London is spluttering and stuttering to a standstill in winter after a lone flurry of snow, New Yorkers are shouting, "Is that all you've got?" The constant deluge is taken in the city's stride: neighbours and shop owners shovel snow; salt is hastily dispatched to make sure pavements don't turn into skating rinks.

Manhattan is just 21km long and a couple wide; diminutive to say the least. You'd imagine that a place so small and packed might become a congealed ball of homogeneity – an American dream on speed. Not so. Indeed, can there be any other metropolis on the planet with so many micro-neighbourhoods, each with a defiantly different look and feel? You can wander just a few blocks in Manhattan – and the same goes for Brooklyn – and feel like you're in a different world. It's often hard to believe that the debonair, refined wealth of the Upper East Side segues (albeit reluctantly) into Spanish Harlem, one of the city's humblest parts.

When people complain about New York I feel the need to defend it. As a Brit I'm an outsider, sure, but I have a sense of what New York is today and how far it has come in its recent history.

In the 1970s New York was a genuinely dangerous Faustian metropolis. By 1975, schools and hospitals were shutting on a regular basis and the city was right on the edge of bankruptcy. Even as recently as the late 1980s the city remained edgy to say the least.

"You'd imagine that a place as small and packed as Manhattan might become a congealed ball of homogeneity – not so"

I once spoke to Paulette Cole, CEO of department store ABC Carpet & Home, about opening in the Flatiron District during this time. Part of the reason the brand was able to command such a huge space was down to the undesirable zipcode. "I remember lots of broken windows when we opened and having my former partner and the dog hang out in the window until we could get it fixed," Cole said. "Back then the area was a shadowy part of the city."

Yet wander around this busy, desirable shopping district today and it's hard to believe that such an era ever existed.

There are those who hanker after the grittier city of yesteryear, bemoaning the creeping gentrification that has spread beyond Manhattan to Brooklyn and on to

Evolving 'hoods
—

01 Bedford-Stuyvesant
Starting to see plenty of great
restaurants and bars emerging.

02 West Village
Where Manhattan's mad
rush subsides.

03 Dumbo
Micro neighbourhood
between Brooklyn and
Manhattan bridges.

Queens. Detractors claim that middle-class professionals are sapping the life out of the city; that diversity is being sacrificed. The argument has some validity – and care is needed to ensure neighbourhoods hold on to their spark – but only some.

A more positive slant would be to look at how gentrification has breathed new life into once semi-derelict areas (Manhattan's Tribeca being a prime example). If it's handled correctly, regeneration can give an area added economic impetus and that can mean more jobs for the community.

Although I came to this city well into the 21st century, I certainly don't long for a New York of high crime, unsafe public transport and no-go areas. While I'm not about to wander through the most deprived parts of the city late at night, New York feels safe. You can go and have a slice of pizza at Roberta's in Bushwick, Brooklyn, or head up to the furthest reaches of Harlem for some live music; unthinkable suggestions a relatively short time ago.

This more secure environment can only be a good thing; more of the city is there to be discovered than ever before. While you may have to dodge a few pavement dawdlers along the way, you have to admit that despite it all, New York just works. — (M)

ABOUT THE WRITER: Ed Stocker is MONOCLE's New York bureau chief. Before making the move in 2014 he was based in Buenos Aires. He's slowly getting used to the weather extremes and power walking and is enjoying the diverse cuisine. He's essentially living the NYC dream (he's even joined the gym).

ESSAY 11

For the love of Upstate
Hudson's growing cache

——

Its past may speak of whaling and the oil industry but with an influx of newcomers with bright ideas, an exciting new future beckons for Hudson, just north of New York.

*by Ann Marie Gardner,
journalist*

Hudson, New York, a two-hour drive north of New York City – proves there is more to "Upstate" than the prevailing idea of Woodstock with its tie dye, ageing musicians and rustic cabins decorated with wooden totem sculptures. Instead, Hudson has emerged as a cultural destination attracting a new creative class of low-key international intellectuals, artists and a fair number of Brooklynites who have migrated here to live – often persuaded to do so after visiting for a weekend.

As a former Hudson business owner and resident for almost 15 years I have witnessed a dramatic change in Hudson, from a noticeable increase in year-round foot traffic that starts each Thursday night to a jump in property prices and a change in the quality and diversity of the restaurants and shops. The demographic has noticeably transformed in that time, too. For decades Hudson was not a place for families due to drugs, high crime and the bad reputation of the local school system.

Despite the earlier pioneers who moved to the city and restored run-down mansions (regardless of all the problems), the major change came about five years ago. I remember the moment: seeing a young, fashionable couple walking with a pram down the main drag of Warren Street (it was surprising enough for me to have to stop and stare).

It was not long before more twenty-somethings with dramatic facial hair arrived and it became a common occurrence to see writer Malcolm Gladwell, chef Mario Batali and artist Marina Abromovic in the coffee shop. Sadly, the last two dive bars in town were casualties of this boom. My co-workers used to go to the secret bar at the Warren Inn and wake the bartender (who snoozed on the bench with his cat) when they needed drinks. The dive bar and hotel was bought by the folks behind Manhattan's Tribeca Grand Hotel.

The good news is that Hudson is reframing the conversation

Businesses to watch in Hudson
⎯
01 Ornamentum
Top contemporary jewellery.
02 Hawkins New York
The celebrated design company's Hudson home.
03 Mexican Radio
This Mexican restaurant also has an original outlet in New York.

about how to live and work outside urban hubs. Hudson refers to itself in publicity as "Upstate's downtown".

The workforce is re-energised but perhaps not in the traditional sense (very few corporations have a presence here). New residents are instead going for a more creative approach to generating work. They're opening restaurants, bakeries, galleries and food halls. I can think of at least four recent transplants who have bought buildings where they have a shop at street level and live upstairs. Property has always been a good investment and there are more people from all over the world betting on the lucrative housing market here to make a life in Hudson.

So what exactly is so great about Hudson? Sometimes it feels dead and empty and you wonder what all of the fuss is about. But the imperfection and rawness, the mix of historic and run down, the random mix of locals and weekenders grows on you over time. It's a quirky town, so smack in the midst of change it feels like you're watching it live. Plus the Hudson Amtrak train pulls right into town alongside an adorable, historic station at the Hudson River boat launch (and it's walking distance from all the shops and restaurants). There is a world-class wine shop as well as bakeries, restaurants and bars whose food is supplied by surrounding farms. There are top-notch universities nearby (Vassar, Bard and RPI), bald eagles to marvel at and skiing, hiking and waterfalls. Not to mention the weekend flow of people that keeps the downtown culture feeling fresh. Plus the light here has inspired painters for centuries.

"Hudson's imperfection and rawness, the mix of historic and run down, the random mix of locals and weekenders grows on you"

With its community of creative expat New Yorkers who want to live and work here, Hudson has all the ingredients to become the East Coast centre of creative tech; what Silicon Valley is to San Francisco, Hudson could be to New York.

But there is even more of an untapped opportunity and that is the river. Because of its deep harbour, Hudson was a thriving inland port for whaling ships from Nantucket during the end of the

18th century. Today the Hudson River is a key waterway for transporting oil. According to the local newspaper, the *Register Star*, "About 75 per cent of home-heating oil consumed in the United States is consumed in the northeast and, of that, 90 per cent travels by barge." The Hudson moves some 25 million gallons down the river each week.

From my kitchen window I can see the tankers coming down the river. Most often it's a tanker named *Afrodite*. It's magnificent to watch such a huge ship navigate this fairly narrow river, especially through the ice channel in winter. I read that *Afrodite* carries 9.6 million gallons of crude oil down the Hudson and then travels north up the coast to Saint John, New Brunswick.

Upstate has come a long way from the iconic drug-fuelled music festival of the 1960s that not only defined hippie culture but in many ways came to represent the experience of living here. I'm all for welcoming in a new upstate state of mind. — (M)

i

ABOUT THE WRITER: Ann Marie Gardner was MONOCLE's first New York bureau chief before she had the good sense to move to the Hudson Valley. Founder of *Modern Farmer* magazine, she now runs the Tall Dark and Hudson content studio.

ESSAY 12

Let it flow
New York Harbor

The waterways of this city were once choked with the vessels and victuals of the maritime industry. While they are much less prevalent now, their vestiges can still be spotted floating up and down the Hudson.

by Robert Wright, journalist

Waterside bike rides

01 Shore Parkway Greenway
Head to Bay Ridge then ride under the Verrazano Bridge.
02 Hudson River Greenway
From the Battery up to Inwood.
03 East River Greenway
Watch the dramatic currents around Hell Gate.

On 17 January 1524, Giovanni da Verrazzano, an Italian explorer, came upon a surprise. Exploring what he had taken to be a bay, he suddenly found the shores around his vessel spreading out again into a huge pool, protected by the surrounding land and islands. It was New York Harbor.

Anyone who has peered south from Brooklyn Bridge can appreciate the scale of the discovery. But were it not for another piece of water, New York might have remained just another East Coast port, a Boston or Baltimore. It is the wide river stretching north into the distance that made New York a great US maritime centre.

After engineers in 1825 completed the Erie Canal linking the Hudson to the Great Lakes, the timber and grain of the Midwest met Europe's cotton and machinery in New York. Today the converted warehouse buildings of the Lower East Side and West Village testify to the explosive growth that ensued. New York was suddenly making the products arriving from both directions into something new, storing and repackaging the moving goods and financing the whole enterprise.

Many assume that the working days of the Hudson and harbour are over. This is largely the doing of Malcolm McLean, an entrepreneur who in 1956 first loaded containers onto a converted tanker in Port Newark, New Jersey. Ports handling goods in containers required more land than Manhattan or Brooklyn could provide. The cranes that steer those goods now poke up from the skyline on the harbour's New Jersey shore.

But the barge tows that chug past the George Washington Bridge testify to the Hudson's continuing role. Some crude-oil trains from North Dakota unload in Albany, with barges carrying their cargo downriver to New Jersey's refineries. Meanwhile, a bike ride along Brooklyn's Shore Parkway Greenway to the Verrazano Narrows, the strait between islands Staten and Long, shows how vigorous traffic to the wider port remains. Tankers and container vessels steam under the mile-long suspension bridge every few minutes.

Back north, towards Manhattan, lies a vista across one of the great natural harbours. It's easy to imagine the awe that must have gripped an Italian explorer that day nearly five centuries ago. — (M)

ABOUT THE WRITER: Robert Wright, the US industry correspondent for the *Financial Times*, has lived in Brooklyn and worked in Manhattan since 2012. He loves to explore the city on bicycle, zipping over the Manhattan Bridge towards the smell of Chinese food.

Culture
—— High-brow
highlights

The list of revered cultural institutions in New York is seemingly endless, from the Museum of Modern Art and the Guggenheim to the Metropolitan Museum of Art (the latter gargantuan offering making London's British Museum look positively diminutive). There are galleries galore, world-class art collections and top music venues, from grungy dives to tiny jazz joints via art deco slices of entertainment history.

There's always something happening here: a weekday ballet performance at Lincoln Center perhaps or a more leisurely stroll around the Brooklyn Museum at the weekend (and a peruse of the nearby farmers' market while you're at it).

If you want a break from the city there are excellent cultural offerings no more than an hour away. Keep informed every inch of the way by flicking through the city's magazines, listening to local public radio or thumbing the granddaddy of all newspapers, the *New York Times*.

Cinemas
Big-screen icons

① Angelika Film Center,
Soho
Discerning choice

Housed in the Cable Building where Soho meets Noho, this is a relic from an era when today's mega cineplexes were nowhere to be found. On the corner of West Houston and Mercer Streets, the cinema is held in high regard by discerning filmgoers and finicky eaters. While viewing an art-house film you can also choose from a menu of freshly made bistro food. The espressos are great too, which may just help to get you through the more obscure indie flicks.
18 West Street, NY 10012
+1 212 995 2570
angelikafilmcenter.com

(2)
IFC Center, West Village
State of the arthouse

IFC was opened in the West Village in 2005 at the same site as the historic Waverley screen. Owned by the AMC television network – which has an art-house film channel of the same name – this is an establishment that takes its alternative film seriously (every November it hosts New York's documentary festival Doc NYC). Look out for Weekend Classics (which does what it says on the label) and Waverly Midnights, which features late-night films on Fridays and Saturdays. All can be watched while nibbling on organic popcorn.
323 Avenue of the Americas, NY 10014
+1 212 924 7771
ifccenter.com

Crosby Street Hotel
Screening Room, Soho
Club classics

With leather seats made by Italian manufacturer Poltrona Frau and a state-of-the-art 2D/3D digital cinema system with 7.1 surround sound, this private cinema in Soho is truly impressive. Equipped with a small bar and several private-event rooms, this is a glamorous stomping ground where Hollywood stars attend screenings of their latest films. But it is also a forum for independent projects with frequent events open to the public. The Film Club serves dinner or cocktails on Sundays.
79 Crosby Street, NY 10012
+1 212 226 6400
firmdalehotels.com

Nite rider
We love the fish tacos and calamari

(4)
Nitehawk, Williamsburg
Licence to thrill

Lit up like an LED domino set at night thanks to a vivid façade, this independent Williamsburg cinema can also claim its own slice of New York history: it was instrumental in getting a Prohibition-era alcohol ban in cinemas overturned not long after it opened in 2011. Which means that yes, this venue serves the hard stuff while you enjoy a film (there are small tables next to seats inside the screening rooms, as well as servers). Its three screens show an excellent selection of films and with its restaurant pairing food with movies, it's an attractive proposition.
136 Metropolitan Avenue, NY 11249
+1 718 384 3980
nitehawkcinema.com

(5)
Film Forum, Greenwich Village
Alternative vision

Opened as an indie screening space 45 years ago, Film Forum has survived the onslaught of bigger chains and America's taste for blockbusters – in fact this is now the city's only remaining non-profit cinema. Films are selected to provide an unconventional alternative to more commercial fare, from black-and-white classics to foreign flicks. There are three screens open year round and it's also worth checking out the regular talks and special screenings it puts on, as well as the shop with its back catalogue of rare and lesser-known numbers.
209 West Houston Street, NY 10014
+1 212 727 8110
filmforum.org

New York on film

01 Annie Hall, 1977: Eternal characteristics of New York life are captured in Woody Allen's classic: awkward dating scenes, idiosyncratic characters, infectious fun, cosmopolitanism and love that crosses boundaries. Anywhere else it would be impossible.

02 Goodfellas, 1990: With characteristic realism, Martin Scorsese follows the rise and fall of gangsters from an Italian-American neighbourhood in Brooklyn. This mobster New York of drugs, family crime, corruption and glamour may be fictional but it left an indelible imaginative mark.

03 Breakfast at Tiffany's, 1961: The climb from impoverished talent to socialite is as alluring and improbable today as it was when Audrey Hepburn acted out the dreams of a beautiful debutante with expensive taste and humble means in early 1960s New York.

Woody, how about this for your next movie: 'Annie Owl'

①

Moma, Midtown and
Moma PS1, Queens
Game changer

New York has a ridiculous wealth
of museums but Moma, opened
in 1929, houses the world's finest
collection of modern art. Gawk at
the sheer amount of iconic art on
its walls, pieces that you've seen
in documentaries or on postcards.
Lichtenstein, Pollock, Monet,
Bacon, Rousseau: the list goes on.

With a constant roster of new
exhibitions spanning mediums as
diverse as architecture, photography
and sculpture, the breadth of this
museum is overwhelming. Be sure
to check out the Uniqlo Friday
nights (16.00 to 20.00) when free
tickets are handed out.

If you're feeling more adventurous,
head to Queens where PS1, Moma's
sister museum, is located. The
focus here is on contemporary
art, extending into music and
performance that features the likes
of James Turrell and Keith Sonnier
in the permanent collection. Like
Moma's The Modern, PS1 also
features an excellent restaurant
(M Wells Dinette) and in summer
months there's often an organic
garden patch on the roof, leaving
you rather spoilt for choice.
11 West 53rd Street, NY 10019
+1 212 708 9400
moma.org;
22-25 Jackson Avenue, NY 11101
+1 718 784 2084
momaps1.org

Popular art
——
Three million
people visit
Moma each
year

The New Museum, Nolita
Shining beacon

Situated on Bowery since 2007, the New Museum is daring in its art and architecture. The seven-storey building, designed by Tokyo architecture firm Sanaa to look like a series of stacked boxes, reflects daylight as ephemerally as it shines at night. The collection inside comprises 1,000 artworks and the museum has a reputation for scouting global talent: South African painter William Kentridge and Cuban artist Ana Mendiete got their breakthroughs here. Also look out for urban-renewal festival Ideas City.
235 Bowery, NY 10002
+1 212 219 1222
newmuseum.org

2
The Rubin Museum of Art, Chelsea
Eastern promise

Home to a 2,000-strong collection of art from the Himalayas and surrounding regions, the Rubin Museum of Art is unrivalled. What was once New York's flagship Barneys store was transformed in 2014 into a peaceful temple by philanthropist couple Shelley and Donald Rubin, who kept the six-storey spiral staircase by Andrée Putman. Exhibitions range all the way from ancient to contemporary art; on Friday nights admission is free and the café turns into a lounge with live music.
150 West 17th Street, NY 10011
+1 212 620 5000
rubinmuseum.org

3
The Guggenheim, Upper East Side
Shapely shrine

Although not initially keen on building in the Big Apple, architect Frank Lloyd Wright went ahead with the design of this modernist masterpiece next to Central Park on Manhattan's Upper East Side. The museum – all mid-century lines and curves – has played host to an assortment of international exhibits. Make your way up the interior ramp that spirals towards the pinnacle and marvel at the atrium: unlike other museums, there are no dividing sections here – all works are displayed together.
1071 5th Avenue, NY 10128
+1 212 423 3500
guggenheim.org

4
Queens Museum,
Flushing Meadows
City-wide diversity

The Queens Museum is located in one of the few extant buildings from New York's 1939 World's Fair. After a sweeping renovation by architect Rafael Viñoly in 1994 it now boasts a diverse programme ranging from a permanent collection of objects and ephemera from the 1939 and 1964 New York World's Fairs to travelling art exhibitions. Queens is one of the most culturally varied urban areas in the world and the museum dedicates much of its schedule to this diverse audience.
New York City Building, Flushing Meadows Carona Park, NY 11368
+1 718 592 9700
queensmuseum.org

Brooklyn Museum, Prospect Heights
Column conversion

The Brooklyn Museum's beaux arts, fin de siècle building is a statement in itself but we're also fans of the Rubin Pavilion and Lobby: a glass-and-metal renovation that gave the building a new entrance directly under its original Ionic columns. Exhibitions here are often unusual – the museum has covered the history of the high heel, for example – and it has one of the world's best Egyptian art collections. An excellent weekend spot, it's also close to Prospect Park and its Saturday farmers' market.
200 Eastern Parkway, NY 11238
+1 718 638 5000
brooklynmuseum.org

Window on the art world

Lincoln Center is a colossal arts venue on the Upper West Side that includes music halls, an opera house, a library and a theatre. Be sure to swing by in the evening when the vast windows are lit up to reveal artwork by Marc Chagall.
lc.lincolncenter.org

Public galleries
Art for art's sake

① Neue Galerie, Upper East Side
European influence

Art collector Ronald Lauder and exhibition organiser Serge Sabarsky enjoyed a 30-year friendship and a shared love for modern German and Austrian art. Following Sabarsky's death in 1996, Lauder decided to turn their passion into a reality and established the Neue Gallery, housed in the beautiful William Starr Miller mansion on the edge of Central Park, in 2001.

"Everything from the paintings on our walls to the objects in our Design Shop to the strudel in Café Sabarsky is meant to evoke the worlds of Austria and Germany in the early 20th century," says museum director Renée Price (*pictured*). Inside its grandiose rooms – all wood panelling and marble fireplaces – are exhibitions featuring everything from war posters to paintings by Gustav Klimt's protégé Egon Schiele.
1048 5th Avenue, NY 10028
+1 212 628 6200
neuegalerie.org

⑦ Whitney Museum of American Art, Meatpacking District
Fresh impetus

It was a bold move when the Whitney decided to up sticks and move from its refined Upper East Side home to the Meatpacking District. But few now could disagree that the decision was anything short of a triumph. The "stacked units" feel of Renzo Piano's modernist building is intriguing enough. Then there are the outdoor balconies with artwork and excellent views of the Hudson River. And that's before we've mentioned the indoor galleries jam-packed with pieces by greats including Edward Hopper and Andy Warhol.
99 Gansevoort Street, NY 10014
+1 212 570 3600
whitney.org

Design star

Isamu Noguchi, who died in 1988, was an internationally acclaimed designer and sculptor. In Long Island there's a museum dedicated to his life. It showcases sculptures and drawings by the Los Angeles-born visionary, plus blueprints and models from his interior-design work.
noguchi.org

Art house
—
The six-storey mansion was built in 1914

Out of town

01 Storm King Art Center, New Windsor:
A world away from the concrete jungle of New York (well, an hour's drive), Storm King is a sculpture park set in a 200-hectare estate of rolling hills and woodland. The centre has a regular collection of more than 100 pieces alongside temporary works. Visit in autumn when you can see the changing colours of the leaves.
stormking.org

02 Dia:Beacon, Beacon:
Set in a converted factory on the edge of the Hudson River, this space is arguably as impressive as the artwork on display. The 1929 building is a mixture of steel, concrete and glass with plenty of skylights allowing the artwork to be viewed in natural light. Covering some 28,000 sq m, it opened in 2003 and its collection, which ranges from the 1960s to the present day, is complemented by a busy events programme.
diaart.org

03 Parrish Art Museum, Long Island: This beautiful building on Long Island's southern fork was designed by Herzog & de Meuron. The museum, which has been at its current location since 2012, features some 2,600 works spanning everything from US impressionism to contemporary art. Be sure to check out the excellent collection of works by William Merritt Chase.
parrishart.org

② Aperture Foundation Gallery,
Chelsea
Snap happy

A whitewashed industrial art
space in Chelsea, this gallery was
built on the founding principles
of *Aperture*: a quarterly magazine
then based in San Francisco that
was launched by a small group of
photographers in 1952.

The gallery, which also hosts
travelling exhibitions at spaces
throughout the globe, sets out
to "communicate with serious
photographers and creative people
everywhere" while the historic
quarterly continues to be published
within its walls and acts as a
backbone for the non-profit
foundation. *Aperture* not only
has classic and contemporary

exhibitions at its venue but also
hosts lectures and discussions as
well as workshops for professionals
and those with a love of photography.
The bookshop features the imprint's
publications – from Diane Arbus
chronologies to Paul Strand
monographs – highlighting the
foundation's involvement in
ensuring photography's rightful
place in the art scene.
4F, 547 West 27th Street,
NY 10001
+1 212 505 5555
aperture.org

③ Milk Gallery, Meatpacking District
Life through a lens

Set in the heart of the Meatpacking
District near Manhattan's western
edge, Milk Gallery specialises in
photography, much of it from the
fashion world. The space hosts the
work of renowned photographers
as well as showcases of up-and-
comers, including group shows
by photography students from
art and design college Parsons
The New School for Design.

Expect to see exhibitions from
the likes of Steven Sebring or
something from the archives of
Magnum photo co-operative,
always with a fashion and
pop-culture sensibility and often
referencing the worlds of film or
music. The gallery is part of a
professional studio space that also
puts on events (including during
Fashion Week) under the Milkmade
name. A sun-soak on the terrace in
the summer is a must, too.
450 West 15th Street, NY 10011
+1 212 645 2797
themilkgallery.com

① Petzel Gallery, Chelsea
Lofty ambitions

Petzel Gallery runs about eight
shows a year featuring mostly
mid-career painters. Situated in
the city's art gallery heartland,
the large glass doors of this
converted loft open into a
white, brightly lit space. An array
of contemporary artists – from
pop artist Jeff Koons to New
York-based photographer Cindy
Sherman – have featured on the
walls of this gallery, which has a
second branch in Köln.

Even the gallery has become
part of the exhibition on occasion:
in early 2015 Israeli Yael Bartana
built new walls in the space and
painted them black in order to
project a series of her short films.
456 West 18th Street, NY 10011
+1 212 680 9467
petzel.com

②
Robert Blumenthal Gallery,
Upper East Side
Against the grain

Gallerist Robert Blumenthal has
broken with an older generation
of downtown colleagues to set up
shop on the Upper East Side in
a beautiful turn-of-the-century
townhouse. The original hardwood
floors and brightly lit Georgian
rooms are a refreshing contrast to
Chelsea's converted warehouses.
Paintings – often resting casually
against the walls – change monthly.
In a neighbourhood of established
affluence this gallery is a breath
of fresh air.
1045 Madison Avenue, NY 10075
+1 646 852 6332
robertblumenthal.com

*Taking
pictures
is my first
love. Well,
that and
biscuits*

③
James Fuentes, Lower East Side
Contemporary cool

"We're part of a group of founding
galleries in the Lower East Side,"
says owner James Fuentes.
"We're a deeply rooted fixture
in the neighbourhood." Located
in Delancey Street since 2010
(the gallery was previously in
Saint James Place), the premise
is simple: promote the finest
established and up-and-coming
contemporary talent, spanning
everything from painting to
sculpture. There's often a strong
anthropological bent to the
exhibitions: the gallery has showed
Andy Warhol's eight-hour film
epic *Empire* and also showcased
works from the city's "neo-geo"
movement. The breadth of artists
spans the 20th century and beyond,
from Alison Knowles, born in 1933,
to Amalia Ulman, a relative
whippersnapper born in 1989.
55 Delancey Street, NY 10002
+1 212 577 1201
jamesfuentes.com

**Hammer
time**

Sotheby's in New York,
opened in 1955, is one of
the world's most important
art auction houses. It hosts
some 100 events every year,
including the sale of Edvard
Munch's "The Scream"
in May 2012 for $120m, a
world-record auction price
at the time.

④
David Zwirner, Chelsea
Family affair

Zwirner, the son of a German art
dealer, initially decided to pursue a
music career rather than follow in
his father's footsteps. But the calling
proved too hard to resist and today
he has two venues: one on 19th Street
that opened in 2002 and the other a
five-storey space a block north.
Representing more than 40
artists – including the estates of
Dan Flavin, current artists such as
Richard Serra and Marlene Dumas,
plus new additions – the breadth
of work on show is impressive.
525 West 19th Street, NY 10011
+1 212 727 2070;
537 West 20th Street, NY 10011
+1 212 517 8677
davidzwirner.com

⑤
247365, Lower East Side
Timely addition

In case you're wondering, the
digits stand for the number of
hours in the day and the days in
a week and year. Run by Jesse
Greenberg and MacGregor Harp,
this contemporary gallery runs two
spaces: the first in what insiders
call the Donut District in Carroll
Gardens, Brooklyn, and the second
in Manhattan's Lower East Side.
"We're an artist-run base
working in close collaboration with
emerging artists," says Greenberg.
With the bulk of exhibitions
spanning painting, sculpture, video
and performance, look out for
openings every four to six weeks.
57 Stanton Street, NY 10002
twentyfourseventhreesixtyfive.biz

❶

Smalls Jazz Club, West Village
The place to bebop

Though it might appear like a bit
of a ragtag operation, Smalls has
credibility on its side. This cosy
basement den has a reputation
for a consistent jazz line-up that
spans everything from post-bebop
to traditional swing. The focus is
on the music here: mismatched
chairs seat only a portion of
the crowd.

Staying true to its name means
patrons are within touching distance
of the musicians, who stand on a
Persian-style rug rather than a stage.
The entertainment lasts through
the night on weekends so come
early for the first set around 19.00
or wander in post-midnight to catch
the after-hours session, where you
might get some extra improvisation.
183 West 10th Street, NY 10014
smallsjazzclub.com

**It's a
jazz thing**

The world's biggest jazz
stars have graced New
York's stages and while
Smalls is a classic, it's also
worth heading to Harlem.
Everyone from Duke Ellington
to John Coltrane lived in the
neighbourhood; check out
the National Jazz Museum or
Minton's jazz club.

②
Bowery Ballroom, Lower East Side
Old-school appeal

Though it may look like an old
barn that houses trains or buses,
the Bowery Ballroom is far more
interesting than that. A staple in the
fast-changing Bowery area that is
the venue's namesake, the hall plays
stage to some of the world's best
performers. While it's nothing
fancy and doesn't have the pomp
that some of the other venues in
town embrace, this place is just
downright cool.

If you're here for a show, arrive
early. The small balcony at the back
of the hall is a great place to grab
a cocktail and sit for the first set.
6 Delancey Street, NY 10002
+1 212 260 4700
boweryballroom.com

❸
Radio City Music Hall, Midtown
Art deco icon

OK, so let's get the negatives out of
the way first: this venue is located
in Midtown which, unless your
business takes you there, isn't
exactly the most soulful part of
New York. But Radio City feels
like it belongs to an earlier showbiz
era; indeed, the beautiful interiors
of this 1930s art deco-and-neon
building are by Donald Deskey
and alone make it worth visiting
(the mural in the Grand Foyer is
the highlight). Fittingly for a venue
of this stature it attracts some of the
world's big names.
1260 Avenue of the Americas,
NY 10020
+1 212 465 6741
radiocity.com

There in spirit
—
Smalls also
streams some
performances
online

④
Brooklyn Academy of Music,
Boerum Hill
Broad spectrum

Brooklyn Academy of Music, or
Bam, has been presenting avant-
garde arts since 1861. The US's
oldest performing-arts centre, Bam
spans contemporary theatre, dance,
music and opera. The multi-venue
cultural destination includes the
four-screen Bam Rose Cinemas and
the Bam Cinématek, showcasing
alternative and independent films
as well as retrospective screenings
and festivals. Arrive early to enjoy a
drink at lounge and bar Bam Café
Live, which features free live music
on summer weekends.
30 Lafayette Avenue, NY 11217
+1 718 636 4100
bam.org

I've got
rhythm,
soul and a
dry mouth

Take the floor
Rough Trade
boasts 1,400
sq m of retail
space

⑤

Rough Trade, Williamsburg
From across the pond

A mainstay of London's
independent music scene, Rough
Trade opened a New York venue
in Brooklyn in 2013, making it the
city's largest record shop. Housed
in a former film-prop warehouse,
this multilevel space is built out of
old shipping containers comprising
a shop floor, installation gallery,
in-house café in collaboration with
Brompton Bicycle Company and a
250-capacity live music venue and
bar. It's a more intimate space than
most in the city with events ranging
from up-and-coming artists to big-
name acts.
64 North 9th Street, NY 11249
+1 718 388 4111
roughtrade.com

Best of the rest
New York media round-up

Radio: essential listening

01 Marketplace: Host Kai Ryssdal has a knack for making finance and business intriguing. This half-hour evening show explains everything from debt woes to the science behind sports betting in one hit. One thing's for sure: if you've any interest in the quirky side of US economics, this show, which is available on WNYC, is for you.
marketplace.org

02 Food Talk with Mike Colameco: OK, so the name is no-frills but this hour-long online culinary radio show cuts through the fluffy, celebrity-driven pomp that other food media in the US seem to proliferate. From behind the microphone in Brooklyn pizzeria Roberta's, host Mike Colameco brings decades of New York food-scene experience to listeners, from government food policy to how to cook a perfect sous-vide meal. Refreshing stuff.
heritageradionetwork.org

03 Moth Radio Hour: An attempt to recreate the porch-side chats that host George Dawes Green enjoyed in his native Georgia, the *Moth* started off with a group of storytellers in Green's living room. Now a global event, its popularity has seen visits to Boston, Seattle, Detroit and Los Angeles as well as London and Dublin. If you can't make it in person, tune in to the weekly show.
themoth.org

①
Magazines
Titles to be proud of

We are thankful for a few magazines that keep the New York media mix fresh. As the name implies ❶ *Gather Journal* focuses on getting people together to discuss topics including organic food or homeware while ❷ *Document Journal* showcases fashion as it relates to Manhattan and surrounding boroughs. And don't let ❸ *Pin-Up*'s oddly designed cover deter you; this biannual "architectural entertainment" publication challenges a few design conventions. To dig a bit further into New York's mag rack pick up a copy of tried and true *New York Times*' *T Magazine* or *New York Magazine*.

②
Kiosks
The rack pack

Don't be fooled by ❶*Casa Magazines*' modest exterior. This West Village shop is well stocked with a fine choice of printed material, including a decent offering of back issues. Elsewhere, the black signage hanging in front of ❷*Bouwerie Iconic Magazine* is a strong indication of what you can expect to find inside this shop: a flawlessly organised international selection. And ❸*Mulberry Iconic Magazines* in Nolita keeps pace with the area's stylish residents, boasting a top selection of hard-to-find publications from around the globe.

WHERE TO FIND THEM
01   Casa Magazines
     22 8th Avenue, NY 10014
     +1 212 645 1197
02   Bouwerie Iconic Magazine
     215 Bowery, NY 10002
     +1 212 420 1004
03   Mulberry Iconic Magazines
     188 Mulberry Street, NY 10012
     +1 212 226 3475

The Monocle Daily

It would be remiss not to mention Monocle 24's own radio show that offers a round-up of world news with a focus on the Americas. Our New York bureau and correspondents across the region ensure that you stay completely up to date.
monocle.com/radio

Design and architecture
—— The apple of your eye

New York is both industrial and industrious. The former because it has always been an important port; the latter because contemporary New York knows how to play this part of its history to its advantage. While the outskirts of the city may still be a little bleak, in Manhattan and Brooklyn – and other outer boroughs – old warehouses have been turned into modern conversions and blended with the city's fascinating hotchpotch of styles.

Indeed, New York's industriousness means you can see everything from art deco to beaux arts edifices (and even a Swedish cottage if you trek into the middle of Central Park). But we're fans of little design details, too: the hidden rooftops, neon signs, wooden benches, water containers and fonts that get below the surface of the metropolis. And then there's all that is above the surface (yes, we're talking about the city's epic skyline). These are the things that make the Big Apple big.

Landscape/outdoor architecture
Special spaces

Hunter's Point South Park
Waterfront Park, Queens
Homegrown success

Enter this vast waterfront park in Long Island City and you may forget you are in one of the globe's busiest metropolises. The formerly abandoned post-industrial space was transformed by a collaborative team of park designers at Thomas Balsley Associates and Weiss/Manfredi, alongside infrastructure architecture firm Arup. Boasting impressive views of Manhattan, the park is flush with native greenery as well as a mix of sustainable wood and concrete; its open space includes a central circular field and plaza where there is a 1,200 sq m pavilion and elevated café. The site is designed with biofiltration swales spanning its length and is oriented to optimise passive heating and cooling.
Center Boulevard, between 50th and 54th Avenues, NY 11101
nycgovparks.org

2
Rockaway beachfronts, Queens
Riding a wave

Since 2012's Hurricane Sandy left Rockaway Beach ravaged, architects and designers have turned the seaside destination into an example of a world-class restoration. Bold colours and graphics complement modern, resilient design on raised islands now found at 86th, 97th, 106th and 116th streets, where architects from Sage and Coombe have restored buildings. Metal slatted canopies provide mild relief from the sun and wooden steps lead back to the beach – the work of landscape architects at Mathews Nielsen.
Beach Channel Drive, NY 11693
nycgovparks.org

Pier 15 Park, Financial District
Local favourite

Those who frequent this elevated green space can feel like they've cheated the system by getting free access to a wide-open park with city views on all sides. Built atop a pier adjacent to the South Street Seaport, this Shop Architects-designed perch is all but invisible to those strolling along the East River but the complex is a double-decker. Under the park is an educational space and café that fills up during busy summers.

While it doesn't have the same story (or crowds) as the High Line, which means it can lay claim to a more mellow reputation, this is truly a "do as the locals" spot that you shouldn't miss.
South Street, NY 10005
nyharborparks.org

④

The High Line, Manhattan
Top attraction

One of Manhattan's most applauded
recent design successes (and perhaps
a little over applauded at times),
the High Line – opened in 2009
– cleverly kills two birds with one
stone. It helps solve the chronic lack
of green space on the island and has
regenerated a disused raised railway
line, re-envisioned as an urban park
thanks to some nifty landscaping.

The High Line park, filled
with grass, plants and perennials,
runs from Gansevoort Street in
the Meatpacking District to West
34th Street between 10th and 12th
Avenues, with ongoing work to
integrate it into the neighbouring
Hudson Yards regeneration project.
We particularly like the "peel-up"
benches on the last phase of the
High Line, completed at the end of
2014, that will fade from dark wood
to silver patina over time, blending
seamlessly with the new paving
and old tracks.
thehighline.org

New York's home to some real high flyers

Local talent

The modernist Seagram
Building represented an
important passing of the torch
in the history of architecture in
New York. Ludwig Mies van der
Rohe designed the skyscraper
with his protégé Philip Johnson,
the pair jointly working on its
interiors and two restaurants.
Johnson continued making
his modernist mark on New
York with the design of the
David H Koch Theater and his
postmodern turn can be seen
on the skyline in the classically
crenellated Sony Building.

New York architect Richard
Meier also cut his teeth while
working with modernist master
Marcel Breuer, before becoming
known for his whitewashed
1980s residences dotting
the shores of the Hamptons.
Meier's signature minimalism
recently found a home on the
edge of Brooklyn's Grand Army
Plaza with the design of On
Prospect Park, a multistorey
steel-and-glass residential
building, as well as on
Manhattan's West Side with
his stately 173 and 176 Perry
Street towers.

New arrival
Trains ran on
the High Line
for 46 years
until 1980

Citywide graphic design and visual identity
Look and learn

①
Metronome, Flatiron District
Swing on by

Designed by Kristin Jones and
Andrew Ginzel, and dating from
1999, "Metronome" is one of New
York's more mysterious public-
art installations, plastered to the
façade of One Union Square South.
The most intriguing section is a
12-digit electronic display showing
a seemingly random set of numbers
(in fact it's telling you the 24-
hour-clock time to the second
and what's left of the day) that
manages to capture some of the
frenzy and energy of the city.
Undoubtedly a landmark but
one that baffles and delights
New Yorkers in equal measure.
1 Union Square South, NY 10003

Divided loyalties
—
While the Metronome may
divide opinion it's not as
controversial as Aluminaire
House, the US's first all-metal
pre-fabricated house from
1934. It was moved from NYC
to Palm Springs in early 2015
after the city rejected giving it
a permanent home in Queens.

②
New York Times logo
Design classic

This instantly recognisable logo
has been through mild updates
over the years but its first major
change came in 1967 when the
Times dropped the full stop after
its name, previously present for
116 years. The change – hardly
revolutionary – caused uproar and
the paper reportedly lost some 1,000
subscribers. Famed typographer and
native Brooklynite Ed Benguiat was
the man tasked with the update; he
is credited with the design of more
than 600 typefaces and logotypes
spanning *Esquire*, *Reader's Digest*
and Coca-Cola. Benguiat took a
minimalist approach, making his
small changes by hand.
nytimes.com

③
Commissioners' Plan, 1811
Think inside the box

Manhattan's most distinctive urban
characteristic is its grid layout. A
testament to the city's efficiency
and pragmatism, this urban plan
was originally presented in the
form of a sizeable map called the
Commissioners' Plan of 1811.
    The plan allowed for the orderly
development and regulated sale
of land in Manhattan across the
axes of 12 north-to-south avenues,
eventually intersected by over 100
numbered streets. You can view
a reproduction of the map in the
book *The Greatest Grid: The Master
Plan of Manhattan 1811–2011*.
Alternatively, urban-planning buffs
can view a 3D panorama of New
York's topography and its 895,000

buildings (built up until 1992)
at the Queens Museum of Art.
*Queens Museum of Art,
Flushing Meadows Corona Park,
NY 11368
queensmuseum.org*

④
Street signage
Glowing endorsement

Visitors often flock to Times
Square to see the brightest and
loudest digital signage but old-
time New York is most elegantly
spelled out on its waterfront. Take
a meander over the Queensboro
Bridge on the Upper East Side
to spy the two-storey red neon
sign for the city's largest film-
and-television studio, Silvercup,
enterprisingly looming above
the bridge's overpass. Crossing
the East River into Long Island
City, Queens, you can cheers the
Pepsi-Cola sign recently moved
from a nearby site. It's calligraphic
neon offering from 1936, complete
with a classic bottle, faces the UN
building across the water.
    Back in Manhattan and looking
onto the Hudson River, the New
Yorker Hotel on 34th Street
announces itself in outsized, blocky
neon red letters atop its 1930s art
deco massing, visible from the
northernmost stretches of the
High Line park.

6
I love NY logo
Heart of the city

Back in the late 1970s, high crime and corruption made New York a place to avoid. With lofty aims of rebranding it as place of pride, the city contracted an advertising firm. It, in turn, hired Milton Glaser to come up with a new brand identity for the metropolis. With pop-art impact, Glaser created a simple text block with the easily replicated proclamation: I Love NY. The design is now on everything from T-shirts and coffee mugs to mobile-phone cases and skateboard decks. You can see the original concept sketch and storyboards in the Museum of Modern Art.
moma.org

Milton Glaser's logo first appeared in 1977

5
Subway typography
Underground talent

Few graphic designers have their work viewed so many times on a daily basis as Massimo Vignelli. One of the Italian designer's most celebrated works is the New York subway map and iconography, which debuted in 1972. The designer worked alongside Bob Noorda at the Unimark design firm; together they organised the previously chaotic signage.

The result was so celebrated that it has been included in the Museum of Modern Art's collection of postwar design. Details of the Helvetica shift – a series of clean and colourful letters and numbers – were printed in a 174-page manual that still guides signs made today. While Vignelli's first streamlined map was redrawn to be more geographically accurate in 1979, the original diagram can be viewed on the MTA's Weekender section on its website.
web.mta.info/weekender

7
Anthora cup
Hot seller

New York and coffee are indivisible. One of the first immigrant communities to promote the brew in the city was Greek and by the 1960s they boasted a formidable network of cafés and diners. Leslie Buck, owner of Sherri Cup Company, smelled a business opportunity and in 1963 designed a paper cup, the Anthora, which he hoped to sell to Greek hospitality clients. The design in blue and white (the colours of the Greek flag) featured kitsch classical motifs and included the slogan "We are happy to serve you". It would prove an instant hit, resonating well beyond the Greek community.

In 1994, 500 million Anthoras were sold in a year

Transport buildings
Positive momentum

A.D. 1908

1

Battery Maritime Building,
Financial District
All aboard

Taking cues from its beaux arts
transport brethren uptown (Grand
Central Terminal et al), the Battery
Maritime Building stands in stark
contrast to the newly built Staten
Island Ferry terminal next door.
Seen from the water, high arches of
stucco, steel, cast iron and ceramic
tiles accentuate the building's three
mooring stations. A green hue
provides a welcome bit of colour
against the backdrop of the ever-
changing glass and steel skyline
of Lower Manhattan.

From the street, intricate
wrought-iron designs crawl up the
front of the building. Step inside
and muse at the 800 sq m Great
Hall where ferry passengers used
to await their seaborne transport;
during summer months the
terminal is still used as a departure
point for people headed to nearby
Governors Island.
10 South Street, NY 10004
batterymaritimebuilding.com

Ship shape
—
The ferry
runs 24 hours
a day all
week

② Former City Hall subway station, Financial District
Changing trains

After the Chicago World's Fair in 1893, the City Beautiful movement emerged. The idea was that a city could be both an economic centre *and* aesthetically pleasing. Grand Central Station and Washington Square Park are New York examples but look below ground for another.

Disused since 1945, the former City Hall subway station boasts chandeliers and vaulted ceilings. The New York Transit Museum opens it for a few weekends a year but with tickets scarce, get on a downtown 6 train at Brooklyn Bridge Station and stay onboard for a glimpse as it swaps to the uptown platform.
web.mta.info

③ TWA Flight Center, Queens
Above the rest

Don't let the poorly planned arterial routes at JFK International Airport scare you off before you take a look at the TWA Flight Center. The Eero Saarinen-designed terminal, opened in 1962, is a throwback to a bygone era of travel. From the departures roadway at the newer Terminal 5, onlookers can take in views of this architectural marvel that has been protected by the National Register of Historic Places. Access is tough but for the design-obsessed, a lap around the outside will provide plenty of mid-century curves to gawk at. The space is slated to be transformed into a hotel that will open in 2018.
JFK Airport, NY 11430
twaflightcenterhotel.com

This design legacy is floating my boat

①
The Skyscraper Museum,
Financial District
Tall stories

The skyscraper embodies
New York and the Skyscraper
Museum, located at Manhattan's
southernmost tip in Battery Park,
chronicles the varied history of the
city's most distinctive architectural
form. It can also keep its focus
micro, such as an exhibition on
proposed and built skyscrapers in
Times Square during 1984.

The museum, designed by
Skidmore Owings & Merrill,
features rotating exhibits alongside
a well-stocked book shop. Its
interior resembles a city skyline
with tall, cubic vitrines appearing
to extend infinitely into mirrored
ceilings and floors.
39 Battery Place, NY 10280
+1 212 968 1961
skyscraper.org

On the rise
—
New York
has about 235
skyscrapers

Dinner drama
——
There is also
a restaurant
and theatre
on site

(3)
Cooper Hewitt, Upper East Side
Modern classic

After its major renovation, this
design museum located inside
the Andrew Carnegie Mansion
reopened at the end of 2014. For
its permanent collection of 212,000
objects, the renovated Cooper
Hewitt has added 60 per cent more
gallery space and a redesigned
garden café. The new look also
includes innovative features
such as an "immersion room",
where examples of the museum's
10,000-piece wallpaper collection
can be projected onto the walls.
2 East 91st Street, NY 10128
+1 212 849 8400
cooperhewitt.org

②
The Museum of Arts
and Design, Midtown
Made in New York

Located in a modernist edifice of
glass and metal – it looks like a
collection of Tetris blocks joined
together – this museum has been
promoting design and its offshoots
since it opened in 1956 (albeit in
a different location and under a
different name) with an emphasis
on craftspeople and artisans.
Exhibitions have included an
exploration of design and craft in
Latin America and a retrospective
of US designer Wendell Castle.
The museum also hosts regular
workshops and talks.
2 Columbus Circle, NY 10019
+1 212 299 7777
madmuseum.org

Paper and posters

01 Bowne & Co, Financial District: Stationery shop Bowne & Co has a heritage dating back to 1775. Located inside the South Street Seaport Museum since 1975 (next to its original 18th-century site) and round the corner from Wall Street, the converted dock building is all exposed brick walls and wooden flooring. Master printer Robert Warner mans the shop using a 19th-century Colombian printing press – apparently weighing as much as an elephant – alongside several other machines from the same period. The old ways prove best here; his children's picture stories and maps are essential items. And if you time your visit well, you could be in time for one of the book launches that are regularly held here.
southstreetseaport museum.org

02 Philip Williams Original Vintage Poster Store, Tribeca: Philip Williams Original Vintage Poster Store spans everything from classic French design to Italian films. There are more than 100,000 posters here all sold by Williams, a former art dealer who moved into posters more than 40 years ago. "Posters are great works of art," he says. "You're buying a piece of history and culture but for an inexpensive price." His archives of 500,000 may have museum-like qualities but in this Tribeca haunt you're welcome to dig through the artefacts. Bring a snack; you could be here a while.
postermuseum.com

Hidden treasures
Worth the trek

① Audubon Center at the Boathouse, Prospect Park
Floating palace

For this former boathouse, built in 1905, designers Frank J Helme and Ulrich Huberty took inspiration from Jacopo Sansovino's 16th-century Venetian Library of St Mark to construct a masterpiece. Today it serves as the nation's first urban Audubon Center, an environmental educational location for the residents of Brooklyn. Facing westward by the water, the building catches the daily sunset on its exterior. Secluded among trees by the lake, visitors can quietly admire its meticulous arches, columns and tiles – or bring a picnic to enjoy the surroundings on its front steps.
101 East Drive, NY 11225
+1 718 965 8951
prospectpark.org

The prospect of Prospect Park is quite a... prospect

② The Cloisters, Washington Heights
Piece of history

The charm of this serene medieval-style sanctum in the middle of Manhattan lies not so much in its celebrated unicorn tapestry exhibits, or even the carved stone altarpieces, but the building and surrounding gardens in which they are housed.

In summer the Cuxa Cloister – a 12th-century structure imported from the Pyrenees in southern France – transforms into a radiant sunshine-filled pocket. The soft pinks and greys of its limestone structure are overpowered by rich, lustrous green (in winter the heated arcades transform into a glass-enclosed space). Sheltered inside the chapter house with your eyes closed, it's easy to imagine yourself kicking back with King Arthur and Sir Lancelot.
99 Margaret Corbin Drive, NY 10040
+1 212 923 3700
metmuseum.org

At the pearly gates
—

Pomander Walk isn't the only hidden mews in the city. Another favourite is Grove Court, located just off Grove Street in the West Village. Behind a gate and surrounded by greenery are six petite red-bricked townhouses dating from the 1850s.

③
Pomander Walk, Upper West Side
Little England

Tucked away on the Upper West Side, this beautiful and historic city block might go unnoticed if you're not seeking it out. The private lane between 94th and 95th Streets was inspired by a 1910 play set on a fictitious London street of the same name. Throughout the years the urban hideaway has seen many notable residents pass through, including Humphrey Bogart, Rosalind Russell and Lillian Gish. Though the Tudor-style homes are behind a closed gate, passers-by can glimpse through at the picturesque street and admire its particularly well-kept green spaces.
265 West 94th Street, NY 10025

Architectural icons

01 Grand Central Station, Midtown East: The train station's soaring ceiling features a grand mural restored in the 1990s. Look closely in the northwest corner to see where restorers left a rectangular patch of soot as a reminder of its former state.
grandcentralterminal.com

02 Brooklyn Bridge, Financial District: Brooklyn Bridge Park (located at the bridge's Brooklyn terminus) has risen from being a defunct cargo-ship port to one of the city's most celebrated waterfront public spaces.
brooklynbridgepark.org

03 Chrysler lobby, Midtown East: Opened in 1930, Edward Trumbull's lobby mural in the Chrysler Building called "Transport and Human Endeavor" is an art deco work depicting soaring images of towers, planes in mid-flight and a Chrysler assembly line.
405 Lexington Avenue, NY 10174

04 Flatiron Building, Flatiron District: Revered for its unusual corner site, the upper registers of Daniel Burnham's 1902 building feature flourishes such as reliefs of tragi-comic faces, lions and severely sculpted entablatures.
175 Fifth Avenue, NY 10010

05 Rockefeller lobby, Midtown: In 1932, Nelson Rockefeller asked Communist-aligned Mexican artist Diego Rivera to paint murals at his newly constructed Rockefeller Center. Upon realising their politicised imagery, he hired Catalan artist Josep Maria Sert instead.
rockefellercenter.com

Regeneration projects
Restorations

①
Cacao Prieto, Red Hook
Sugar and spice

On the Brooklyn waterfront, Cacao Prieto houses a rum distillery and chocolate factory in a vast red-brick warehouse. A third of the building is an original 1846 Dutch renaissance-influenced construction (it currently houses the Botanica bar). The adjoining main building from 2007 has been shaped in a similar style by architect Rhett Butler using bricks from demolished sites nearby.

"Modern architecture typifies society's obsession with the superficial requiring periodic facelifts – but in 200 years time Cacao Prieto will still be standing," says Robert Charles Lutz, company sales director and junior distiller.
218 Conover Street, NY 11231
+ 1 347 225 0130
cacaoprieto.com

Sweet success
—
1,000 cacao beans make around 1kg of chocolate

CACAO PRIETO

WIDOW JANE

② Cooper Union, East Village
Elevated position

The adjacent neo-Romanesque Foundation Building and modernist 41 Cooper Square at architecture, art and engineering college Cooper Union indicate just how much the professions taught there have changed since it was founded in 1859. Peter Cooper designed the original building to be the tallest in Lower Manhattan, complete with a shaft housing a pulley system (he was ahead of his time on lifts). As for 41 Cooper Square, Pritzker Prize-winning architect Thom Mayne designed the building with, you guessed it, working lifts.
Cooper Square, NY 10003
+1 212 353 4100
cooper.edu

③ Pier A, Financial District
Harbour intentions

A registered New York landmark, Pier A is located on the water where the Hudson meets Battery Park in Lower Manhattan. The historic building that runs along the promenade – dating back more than 120 years – served as an HQ for the city's harbour police but has recently been remodelled and opened to the public. Restoration work began in 2009 and was completed in the summer of 2013. The interior – all wood and exposed piping – affords excellent sunset views. Now housing a bar and restaurant called Harbor House, an accompanying cocktail is optional.
22 Battery Place, NY 10004
+1 212 785 0153
piera.com

Navigating New York is a walk in the park

(1)

Neo-gothic: Woolworth Building
Early riser

Built in 1913, the Woolworth Building located in the Financial District was the tallest building in the world at the time. Despite its mass, the early skyscraper seems lithe and soaring thanks to architect Cass Gilbert's ribbed mullions that dress its 60 storeys, an early example of neo-gothic style that would go on to characterise the city's first skyscraper boom.
233 Broadway, NY 10007
thewoolworthtower.com

Global thinkers
—
The UN employs 44,000 worldwide

(2)

Mid-century: UN Secretariat building
World-class design

By Manhattan's East River, this towering mass is a prime example of mid-century architecture. It was designed by architecture icons such as Le Corbusier and Oscar Niemeyer and some of the interiors are decked out by Norway's finest mid-century artists.
405 East 42 Street, NY 10017
visit.un.org

Deconstructivism: IAC Building
Shape shifter

Frank Gehry's first building in New York is unmissable from the raised platform of the High Line park, between West 18th and 19th streets. The building has a smooth, rippling form that changes depending on how the light hits it at certain times of day.
555 West 18th Street, NY 10011
iachq.com

(4)

Art deco: General Electric Building
Current favourite

New York's roaring 1920s is exemplified in skyscrapers from the Chrysler Building to the Empire State. Cross & Cross's equally commanding General Electric Building features an ornate crown of decorative limestone that mimics the transmission of electricity.
570 Lexington Avenue, NY 10022

⑤
Beaux arts: New York
Public Library
Literary classic

This was the largest marble edifice
in the country when it opened in
1911, which goes some way to
explaining why it took 12 years to
build. The Stephen A Schwarzman
Building, often referred to as the
"main branch" of the New York
Public Library, is a beaux arts
landmark located a few steps from
Grand Central. It majestically sits
on a large terrace, its entrance
flanked by two large lions by the
names of Patience and Fortitude.
5th Avenue at 42nd Street,
NY 10018
+1 917 275 6975
nypl.org

*Owls
eat book
worms for
dinner*

McGraw Rotunda

SUBLIME

Far out — Documents in the library would stretch to 16km

Sport and fitness
—— Be active

From juice bars to gyms via a run in one of the city's parks, New York is a city that takes exercise and clean living extremely seriously (in among the cocktail debauchery, of course). A jog in Central Park is a given but why not explore one of Brooklyn's lesser-known areas or take on the urban jungle of Lower Manhattan on foot? Indeed, even when you're not formally exercising here you are likely to be powering around on two legs in this most mobile of metropolises.

And while New York may not be officially referred to as bike-friendly (yet) it is making great progress: the Hudson River Greenway, running down the western spine of Manhattan, is one of the world's great urban cycle routes. (Its bike-share scheme isn't too shabby either.)

Swimming pools
Different strokes

Le Parker Meridien pool, Midtown
Swim with a view

This hotel has a few secrets – one of which is Burger Joint. Yes, a hamburger joint slyly hidden behind a curtain in the lobby. It doesn't really match the high-end nature of the hotel but it does intrigue. So too does the pool atop the same property.

It is hard to match a view from high above Central Park but it seems hotel Le Parker Meridien doesn't think just any view (or any burger joint) is enough. The property's indoor pool deck has unobstructed views of the park, allowing swimmers to soak and take in the city at the same time.

Most of New York's rooftop properties go to restaurants or bars, which often means that prime pool space is taken. But not to worry, the folks here thought of everything: a great pool menu means you can enjoy the view while having lunch and then slip right back into the water. And for those wanting to catch some rays there's an outdoor sun deck.

The hotel offers day passes that give you full access to the pool and Gravity Fitness gym. Located under the property, the gym is well equipped for a day of getting your body back in shape – save for the burger you'll likely eat in the lobby.
119 West 56th Street, NY 10019
+1 212 245 5000
parkermeridien.com

② Park Hyatt pool, Midtown
On top of the world

Hotel pools in Manhattan often aren't quite right and you can't blame them: this city wasn't really built to leave room for a grand piscine. Fortunately, those in charge of the Park Hyatt's recent revamp thought grand was the only way to go. Set 25 storeys above the city, a wall of windows gives incredible views from the water. And not just any view: swimmers and loungers get a bird's eye perspective of Carnegie Hall. For those looking to relax, classical music is played throughout the space and even through underwater speakers.

And you don't have to be a guest to use the pool: simply drop into the hotel's Spa Nalai, where certain treatments give you all-day access to the water.
153 West 57th Street, NY 10019
+1 646 774 1234
hyatt.com

I've always been a huge believer in taking a birdbath

Outdoor swimming

01 **McCarren Park Pool, Williamsburg:** Built in 1936, Brooklyn's McCarren Park Pool is a bit of a throwback. After decades of operation, the life of the facility eventually ran its course. For years the grand brick building and pool sat in disrepair as officials looked for ways to bring the publicly owned complex back to life. In 2012 the pool was reopened to the public during the summer to much fanfare.
mccarrenpark.com

02 **Lasker Rink and Pool, Central Park:** At the north end of Central Park sits Lasker Rink and Pool. Don't let the name confuse you: depending on the season it's either a rink or (you guessed it) a pool. In summer months swimmers flock to the mid-century oasis to escape the heat. In winter, forget the bathing suit and rent a pair of skates.
centralparknyc.org

Pinch of salt
The club has eight saltwater pools across the city

New York Health & Racquet Club, Financial District
Downtown detox

If you are downtown and in need of a few flip-turns we suggest you get a day pass to New York Health and Racquet Club's Whitehall Street location. It's not as fancy and doesn't have the views that some of the other pools on our list have but it will give you everything you need to have a good water workout. Once finished in the 18-metre saltwater pool, hop into a whirlpool to give your muscles a break. Or step into the eucalyptus infrared sauna, which is said to help you sweat out the toxins.
39 Whitehall Street, NY 10004
+1 212 269 9800
nyhrc.com

Healthy options

If you don't have the time (or the will) for a bona fide workout there are still a number of ways that New York can help you get your heart rate up.

01 East River Waterfront Esplanade: In 2014 the city opened an outdoor fitness centre along Manhattan's East River. With 12 exercise machines fastened to the ground between the Manhattan and Williamsburg bridges, the mini open-air gym is a great place to take in views of Brooklyn.
nyharborparks.org

02 Citibike: It seems no major city is complete without a bike-share programme these days. Thanks to Citibike, visitors to New York can buy an unlimited day pass and enjoy quick bike trips between points of interest. Built to get you from A to B, the system is a perfect way to help elevate your heart rate. Just don't treat it like a bike rental: if your trip with the bike is more than 30 minutes you get charged extra.
citibikenyc.com

03 Columbus Park basketball courts, Chinatown: It seems only fitting that while in the city you might challenge a team of locals to a game of "hoops". Basketball is about as American as sports can get and the summer months bring places such as Chinatown's Columbus Park to life with sneaker-wearing ball-dribblers raring for a scrimmage. Pay the park a visit, hop onto a court and see how high you can jump.
nycgovparks.org

Yoga
Strike a pose

①

Pure Yoga, Upper East Side
and Upper West Side
Minimal fuss

Pure boasts two studios in New York
on the east and west side of Central
Park. With outposts in Hong Kong,
Shanghai, Singapore and Taipei, it
offers a variety of styles, from *vinyasa*
to hot yoga, *hatha* and the more
traditional *ashtanga* series, alongside
pilates and barre classes. The studios
are made up of a series of courtyards
and lounges, soothingly modern
and minimalist in design.
Pure East, 203 East 86th Street,
NY 10028
+ 1 212 360 1888;
Pure West, 204 West 77th Street,
NY 10024
+ 1 212 877 2025
pureyoga.com

*We can
do the
downward
dog next*

Cycling
Pedal power

①

Hudson River Greenway,
Manhattan
Cycling route

STARTNG POINT:
  Chelsea Waterfront Park
DISTANCE: 20km to Strictly Bicycles
NOTE: Cycling maps are available
  at *bikemap.net*
Riding a bike through the streets
of Manhattan can be intimidating.
Fortunately the city has built
extensive bike paths both through
and around the city, the best
of which is the Hudson River
Greenway that runs from north
to south. We suggest starting off

at **①** *Chelsea Waterside Park* and
heading north towards the George
Washington Bridge. Along the
route you will have great views of
the Hudson River and come nose
to nose with the **②** *USS Intrepid*, a
decommissioned US navy aircraft
carrier that is now a museum. As
you get further up the path the
challenges increase with a few slight
grades and a climb to the bridge.
  Once you cross the bridge you
can exit to the **③** *Palisades Interstate
Parkway* heading north. This is a
good spot to stop and put some air
in your tyres or grab a power bar at
④ *Strictly Bicycles*, a bike shop that
caters to passing riders. If you're
up for more, follow the parkway
for a while. If you're ready for the
return journey just head back the
way you came. It's mostly downhill
from there.

George
Washington
Bridge

New Jersey

Hudson River

Manhattan

Central Park

The
Bronx

Queens

Wheel deal

Christopher Street meets the
Hudson River right where
Waterfront Bicycle Shop is
located in West Village. Far
from the Midtown traffic, it is
a great starting point for a ride
so rent yourself some wheels;
it costs from $15.
bikeshopny.com

Hair care and grooming

01 Shizen Brooklyn,
Williamsburg: This
Japanese import, sister
to The Oversea in Tokyo,
is sparse and cast in
a calming stark white.
The salon's welcoming
atmosphere is matched
by first-rate stylists.
nyshizen.com

02 Three Squares Studio,
Chelsea: Warm wood
tones and a lofty candle-
lit interior make this
venerable Chelsea salon
a well-appointed retreat.
Indulge in an afternoon
coiffe while drinking a
glass of sparkling.
threesquaresstudio.com

03 Freemans Sporting Club
Barbershop, Lower East
Side: Quick and affordable
yet with an attention to
detail that you don't get in
most barbershops. Style-
savvy staff know their craft
and make you feel at ease.
It is almost impossible
not to nod off after one
of their soothing post-
cut hot towels.
freemanssportingclub.com

04 Frank's Chop Shop,
Lower East Side: Aimed
at the "modern gentleman
of leisure", this Lower East
Side spot has a diverse
and loyal clientele who
come back for military-
precision haircuts and
straight-edge shaves. The
shop sells its own range of
caps and garments, too.
frankschopshop.com

05 Harry's Corner Shop,
Greenwich Village:
Harry's is primarily about
well-designed razors and
shaving products but it
also has a barbershop in
Greenwich Village. As well
as its own range, the shop
sells accessories such as
Makr leather goods and
Geneva speakers.
harrys.com/cornershop

Gyms
Where to work out

①
Equinox Printing House,
West Village
River-view workout

If you want to be like the locals
while breaking a sweat, pay a visit
to Equinox's Printing House. This
standout location for the tidy and
ubiquitous Equinox gym brand
spans multiple storeys in a refitted
West Village building.

In the summer a roof-top pool
gives sun-worshipping gym-goers
a sweeping view of the Hudson
River. Why not head outside for a
post-workout run along the water?
A beefy schedule of fitness classes
will get your heart rate up; all you
have to do is show up on time.
421 Hudson Street, NY 10014
+ 1 212 243 7600
equinox.com

Three more

01 Chalk Gyms, Williamsburg:
It's not huge but it does
the trick. If you're trying
to avoid the throngs of
seen-and-be-seen gym
bunnies common at the
big Manhattan facilities
(and you're staying
in Williamsburg), this
boutique fitness offer is
one for you. Chalk's use of
nearby McCarren Park in
the summertime for some
of its classes is a good
way to see the 'hood.
chalkgyms.com

02 Model Fit, Nolita:
Specialising in fitness
for those who walk the
runway, Model Fit's
approach to wellbeing is
certainly unique. Based
on a mix of methods
that includes pilates
and yoga, the workouts
here are intense. The
gym is located in fashion
photographer Terry
Richardson's former
studio. In warmer months,
do some strength training
then head two blocks east
of the studio to the Allen
Street bike path. Grab a
Citibike and head south
to the waterfront for a
warm-down ride.
modelfit.com

**03 Barry's Bootcamp,
citywide:**
There is a reason why so
many people have taken
up a workout regimen at
Barry's. The high-intensity
boot camps are some
of the most challenging
around – but anyone
who goes will tell you it
pays off. With studios
in Chelsea, Noho and
Tribeca – and around the
world – this is a popular
way to get your cardio
workout. Just be sure
you're amply hydrated
before taking it on.
barrysbootcamp.com

Running routes
On your marks

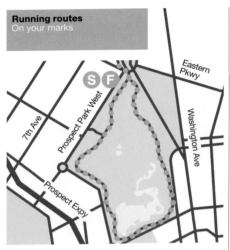

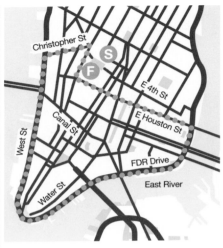

① Prospect Park
Oasis in Brooklyn

DISTANCE: 5.5km
GRADIENT: Flat with a few hills
DIFFICULTY: Mild
HIGHLIGHT: The Prospect Park Boathouse is a great place to sit and stretch out along the pond
BEST TIME: Early mornings and mid-afternoon
NEAREST SUBWAY: Grand Army Plaza

One of the things we really love about Brooklyn's Prospect Park is how imperfect it is in shape. It is the place for a nice running loop of varied elevations and wandering paths. It even has a few trail elements (if that's your thing).

Start your run on the north end of the greenway at Grand Army Plaza. From there follow the path right. At this point it's called West Drive. You'll pass through a few microclimates: grassy meadows, ponds and dense forested patches as you wind through the park.

This run would give you a taste of Brooklyn's diverse districts as it borders multiple, eclectic neighbourhoods. It is easy to feel as though you're part of the community here. Most tourists don't have Prospect Park on their list of sights to see, which makes it a bit of an oasis. To end your run, stop where you started, wander left 50 metres into the centre of the park and stretch in one of the large meadows. Once cooled down, cross to the Prospect Park Zoo (back down East Drive), which happens to be within the park's boundary.

On Sundays families are out in full force and on Saturdays the north end of the park boasts a delightful farmers' market year-round. If you're there on the right day (and during the right season), fresh Hudson Valley produce will await you when you've finished your run.

② Lower Manhattan run
Southern tour of the city

DISTANCE: 12.3km
GRADIENT: Flat
DIFFICULTY: Easy
HIGHLIGHT: Rounding the southern end of Manhattan, where you'll find views of New York Harbor and the Statue of Liberty
BEST TIME: Midday, as most flock here for sunset
NEAREST SUBWAY: West 4th Street – Washington Square

The districts of Lower Manhattan can be a little overwhelming on a map; for a visitor they often merge together. Where does Soho end and Little Italy begin? What does Tribeca stand for? (Head to page 15 for the answer to that one.) It's best to immerse yourself in the local geography. A dash from Greenwich Village's Washington Square Park out to the East River and south around the tip of Manhattan is a good way to assert your neighbourhood knowledge.

To start run south from the park, down MacDougal Street for three blocks until you hit West Houston Street. Turn left and follow West Houston all the way to the East River (it becomes East Houston at a certain point). From there find your way onto the waterfront path and turn right. Stay on that path as it takes you around the tip of southern Manhattan. And keep going.

Once you get to where the Hudson River meets Christopher Street take time for a stretch on the pier. Then follow Christopher Street through the West Village, where you can envy the perfectly restored low-built dwellings and some of the most impressive brownstones in the city. Nearly at the end of your run, pop into Liquiteria on Avenue of the Americas for a smoothie for the warm down (between 8th and 9th streets). This will bring you right back to the park at which you started. Just be sure to look left before crossing the city's busy streets.

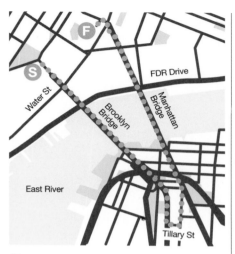

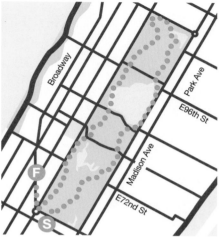

 3

Brooklyn Bridge loop
Sunrise on the East River

DISTANCE: 5.5km
GRADIENT: Mild incline, mostly flat
DIFFICULTY: Easy
HIGHLIGHT: Standing at the centre of Brooklyn Bridge
and the views of Manhattan and Brooklyn
BEST TIME: Early morning, otherwise you're
contending with commuters and tourists
NEAREST SUBWAY: Brooklyn Bridge – City Hall

New York's bridges are often attractions in themselves.
Sure, a New Yorker may pay little mind to the stone-and-
cable grandeur of the Brooklyn Bridge while crossing it
in a car but on foot it can be pretty impressive. There's
no better way to enjoy the landmark than making it part
of a run. Start in front of New York City Hall on the
Manhattan side to Brooklyn. Cross Centre Street and
find the clearly marked footpath.

There are a few caveats to this run. You're most
likely to have your best jog in the morning when there's
less foot and cycle traffic on the bridge. And you can't
beat the view of a sunrise from high above the East
River. Depending on the time of the year, think about
bundling up. A Nike windbreaker could very well be the
perfect accompaniment to your fitness get-up.

Once you have crossed the Brooklyn Bridge the
path will eventually leave you at Tillary Street. Turn left
and walk 400 metres to Flatbush Avenue via Jay Street.
You'll see the Manhattan Bridge on your left. Turn
towards it and find the footpath. Cross the East River
and back again to Manhattan. You'll end up just blocks
from where you began your jog and you'll have killed
two birds (bridges) with one stone. You'll also be in the
heart of Chinatown, which means dim-sum fans have
the perfect place to refuel in the great crimson-and-gold
hall at Jing Fong, a Cantonese cuisine staple.

4

Central Park
Room to move

DISTANCE: 9km
GRADIENT: Hills and flat
DIFFICULTY: Moderate
HIGHLIGHT: The surprisingly big forested curves
to the park's north. It's nice to feel like you've
somehow escaped the city
BEST TIME: Early morning
NEAREST SUBWAY: Columbus Circle

What's not to love about this jog? A runner can access
it at multiple entry points from Midtown to Harlem;
the easiest is at the southwest corner of the park, just 50
metres from the Columbus Circle subway stop. Start
here and follow West Drive left and just keep running
until you're back where you started.

For the serious runner, a loop or two could very
well put you on a training path to the New York City
Marathon. For those less inclined to push it, taking your
time on a journey through Central Park means you can
take stretching breaks in front of the famed Tavern on the
Green, just to the left of West Drive near the start of the
run. Or simply get lost on the winding paths to enjoy the
rock formations and birdwatching.

Back at the Columbus Circle entrance head north
on Broadway to Columbus Avenue. A block up on the
right is Épicerie Boulud: its salads and sandwiches and
outdoor seating make the after-run recharge snappy.

Where to buy

A great spot for all-weather gear is REI (*rei.com*).
For shoes that fit perfectly visit Jackrabbit Sports
(*jackrabbitsports.com*). And for tennies with
street-cred head to Soho's NikeLab (*nike.com*).

Walks
—— Find your
own New York

It's hard to think of a city
that guards its neighbourhood identities quite so
strongly. Crammed onto
the island of Manhattan,
the West Village really
does feel like a charming
hamlet while the Upper
East Side retains an old-
world charm. And Tribeca
has transformed from
downtrodden district
into one of the city's
most coveted residential
spots. In Brooklyn the
same applies, from
Red Hook – with its
saved waterfront – to
flourishing Dumbo.

NEIGHBOURHOOD 01

Red Hook
Industrial revolution

In 2012, superstorm Sandy submerged Red Hook in head-high
water. But the storm is just one chapter in the area's complicated
saga. Its past, riddled with crime, drugs and that destruction of
2012, has given way to a vibrant rethink of the long-dilapidated
industrial district on Brooklyn's southern waterfront.

Now a number of smart and eclectic businesses mark the
promise of this revitalised hood that feels unlike anywhere else in
the city. Getting here is a bit of a hike but some say that keeps
things in order and avoids the neighbourhood being overrun by
the masses. The nearest subway stop is Carroll Street on the F
and G trains, which is a good 25-minute walk away.

Once you arrive you should start at the north end of Van
Brunt Street and work your way south. Be sure to bring your
thirst and appetite because this district is all about food and
drink. You'll pass a number of shops, cafés and restaurants – and
even a plant nursery. The nice thing about a jaunt through this
neighbourhood is that it's mostly a straight shot down one street.

Just a note: if you take all the opportunities to enjoy a tipple
during your stroll, it may become less of a walk and more of a
stumble. If you're still kicking by the end, we salute you.

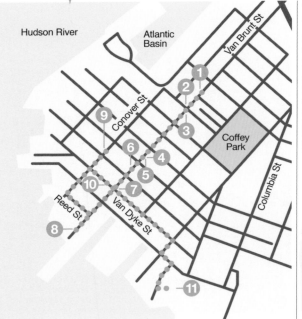

Test the water
Red Hook walk

For a decadent and very American
snack, look for ❶ *Red Hook Lobster
Pound*. It will be on your right.
This place dishes up some of the
best-known lobster rolls outside
New England. Two huge tanks full
of lobsters welcome you as you walk
through the door. But please, keep
your fingers to yourselves. To wash
it all down, wander a few doors
along to ❷ *Red Hook Bait & Tackle*.
Were it not for the bizarre collection

Getting there

Red Hook isn't the most accessible place in New York, which is part of the reason it has retained its charm: the nearest subway stop is about a 25-minute walk away (Carroll Street on the F and G trains). Or get off earlier at Jay Street-MetroTech and get the B61 bus.

of mid-century furniture and taxidermy, this bar might come off a bit differently (read: divey). The knick-knacks and wall signs might make things feel cluttered but somehow there's a method to the madness. If not for a drink, just go to look at all the oddities within.

On the next block on Van Brunt Street is ③*Home Made*. Once a homeware shop and now a café, it focuses on brunch but has an extensive wine list. Peek inside and put this cosy food nook on your list of places for later. Walk another few blocks down Van Brunt Street and on your left is ④*Gallery Brooklyn*. This space marks a solid and smart departure from its fancy brethren elsewhere in the city. Once you're done taking in some art, pop across the street to café ⑤*Baked*. Oddly, an antler takes the place of the doorknob on the front door; just one of the reasons that this café and bakery stands out. Resisting the urge to buy one of the pastries sitting behind the glass is tough.

Keep strolling and you'll happen upon ⑥*Foxy & Winston*. This stationery and textile store is

anything but your ordinary paper shop. Part studio and part retail space, it turns out carefully designed goods with a fun and detail-oriented eye.

Once you've selected your pens and pencils, step back onto the street and turn right. If the weather is warm, make a pit stop at ⑦*Dry Dock Wine & Spirits* to grab a bottle of rosé. We'll tell you why in a second.

At this point you're near the end of Van Brunt Street where you'll find Fairway Pier. Jutting out into the harbour, the cement promenade is quite a place to take it all in. If you walk west along the path you'll end up in a newly developed green space that sits atop a quiet beach. Find a seat anywhere along the water and watch the sun set behind the Statue of Liberty and if you want a picnic, the adjacent ⑧*Fairway Market* has all the trimmings. If you don't, you'll just have to enjoy that bottle of rosé, *sans* nibbles.

It's safe to say that if you've taken all the spots to indulge in libations during this neighbourhood jaunt then perhaps a cold drink of water rather than continuous waterside drinking might now be in order. But those with firmer constitutions can head back north on Conover Street, where a couple more establishments such as distillery and chocolatier ⑨*Cacao Prieto* have put down roots. And step into ⑩*Saipua* for handmade olive-oil soap: a great present for those back home. Or if you're ready to call it a day head east on Beard Street to the Erie Basin Park in front of Ikea; there you can hop on a ⑪*ferry* back to Manhattan's South Street Seaport.

Address book

01 Red Hook Lobster Pound
284 Van Brunt Street,
NY 11231
+1 718 858 7650
redhooklobster.com

02 Red Hook Bait & Tackle
320 Van Brunt Street,
NY 11231,
+1 718 451 4665
redhookbaitandtackle.com

03 Home Made
293 Van Brunt Street,
NY 11231
+1 347 223 4135
homemadebklyn.com

04 Gallery Brooklyn
351 Van Brunt Street,
NY 11231
+1 347 460 4063
gallerybrooklyn.com

05 Baked
359 Van Brunt Street,
NY 11231
+1 718 222 0345
bakednyc.com

06 Foxy & Winston
392 Van Brunt Street,
NY 11231
+1 718 928 4855
foxyandwinston.com

07 Dry Dock Wine & Spirits
424 Van Brunt Street,
NY 11231
+1 718 852 3625
drydockny.com

08 Fairway Market
500 Van Brunt Street,
NY 11231
+1 718 254 0923
fairwaymarket.com

09 Cacao Prieto
218 Conover Street,
NY 11231
+1 347 225 0130
cacaoprieto.com

10 Saipua
147 Van Dyke Street,
NY 11231
+1 718 624 2929
saipua.com

11 Ikea Ferry Shuttle
Ikea Dock, 1 Beard Street,
NY 11231
nywatertaxi.com

NEIGHBOURHOOD 02

Tribeca
Quiet success story

As waterfront neighbourhoods go, few are as pleasantly sequestered as Tribeca, whose boundaries comprise bustling Canal Street and Hudson River Park. Once home to one of the nation's largest outdoor produce markets, the former "butter and eggs" district has undergone quite a transformation in the past 20 years. A prime example is the 145-unit tower by Swiss firm Herzog & de Meuron, nicknamed "the Jenga building" by locals for its wobbly, stacked appearance, which has attracted deep-pocketed tenants.

Though it lacks a discernible main drag (à la Soho's Broadway, for example), the fun here is in the finding: a stroll down Church Street might reveal an artisanal bakery hidden inside an old office building, for example. Or pacing the boardwalk along the river you'll come across Pier 25, home to a miniature golf course. The quiet cobblestone side streets are refreshingly void of rumbling traffic and its arsenal of green oases (the triangular Bogardus Plaza is a favourite) ensures visitors never have to wander too far to sit and relax.

During the week, Tribeca can feel dominated by business types and at the weekend it can seem oddly quiet. Take your walk on a Saturday or Sunday – you'll feel like you have the place to yourself.

Street smart
Tribeca walk

Start your morning at the unconventional ❶ *Arcade Bakery*, whose cosy seating alcoves line the ground-floor passageway of an old office building. Warm, buttery croissants, thin-crust pizzas and cinnamon sugar brioche are the creation of former Bouley Bakery chef Roger Gural. Maybe this is where you head after you've tapped into your chakras at Kula Yoga Project, just four blocks south of the bakery.

After breakfast take a three-minute stroll up Church Street to ❷ *Aire Ancient Baths*. This spa follows the Roman system of using different temperature baths (proceed into the frigidarium at your own risk) but, unlike in Roman times, bathing suits are required. Visits to the unisex bathhouse are booked in 90-minute sessions. After a good soak you head down to Reade Street's ❸ *Nish Nush*. This sit-down or takeaway lunch spot offers a refreshing alternative to the usual *shawarma* joint.

What's clear in Tribeca is that there are plenty of places to eat but it's also not lacking when it comes to places to shop. To dip into the district's retail world, return to Church Street and turn right on Warren Street. Chefs swoon over the blades at Japanese knife shop ❹ *Korin* but there's more than just highbrow cutlery to admire here: sushi-making paraphernalia, chopstick rests and porcelain steam pots only add to the kitchen cred. And don't worry: being a sushi guru isn't obligatory.

Walking north on West Broadway you'll pass one of New York's oldest hotels: the Cosmopolitan. Make your way west to Greenwich Street and walk north along Washington Market Park until you reach ❺ *Carini Lang*. This airy, pillared showroom places its signature product front and centre: richly patterned, hand-woven rugs. The vivid (and often extremely detailed) designs use natural, plant-based dyes and high-quality fibres such as highland wool, silk and mohair.

After giving your home a good once-over it's time for a wardrobe

top-up at ⑥*ManuelRacim*, a French boutique specialising in made-to-measure shirts.

If the shopping spree has put you in the mood for a drink, head south past Duane Park (a tiny but charming green oasis) to where it meets Duane Street. There you will spy "Lappin Tea Co" written in faded white letters along a building's façade: a quaint reminder of Tribeca's past as a bustling mercantile hub. Continue straight to find ⑦*Weather Up*. Gleaming white tile ceilings and a copper bar reflect the warm glow of this Brooklyn transplant. This is a great spot for a midday rest from summer's heat or winter's cold.

Once your whistle's been wetted, walk north on West Broadway and take a left at Franklin Street where you'll find ⑧*Urban Archaeology*. This purveyor of old clocks, decorative bronze railings and shiny bathroom fixtures has built a wide following. In addition to the salvaged artefacts – many sourced from such venerable addresses as the Plaza Hotel – the company specialises in manufacturing vintage-inspired items.

Now head to ⑨*Best Made*, a few blocks east. This brand straddles the unconventional line between utilitarian boutique (lightweight anoraks, heavy woollen sweaters and Pendleton blankets) and art space.

At this point you're likely in need of something caffeinated. If so, point yourself northwest in order to find Debrosses Street, turning right when you reach Washington Street. There you'll see ⑩*Fika*, a relaxed café and chocolate factory with a small but satisfying lunch menu of Swedish-inspired dishes.

Getting there

The M5 bus runs to the closest stop to the start of your walk at Church and Thomas Streets but there are plenty of subway stations within five or 10 minutes: try the A/C/E station at Canal Street or take the 1/2/3 train to Chambers Street, which puts you closer to the heart of Tribeca.

Address book

01 Arcade Bakery
220 Church Street,
NY 10013
arcadebakery.com

02 Aire Ancient Baths
88 Franklin Street,
NY 10013
+1 212 274 3777
ancientbathsny.com

03 Nish Nush
88 Reade Street,
NY 10013
+1 212 964 1318
nishnushnyc.com

04 Korin
57 Warren Street,
NY 10007
+1 212 587 7021
korin.com

05 Carini Lang
335 Greenwich Street,
NY 10013
+1 646 613 0497
carinilang.com

06 ManuelRacim
44 Hudson Street,
NY 10013
+1 212 233 0417
manuelracim.com

07 Weather Up
159 Duane Street,
NY 10013
+1 212 766 3202
weatherupnyc.com

08 Urban Archaeology
143 Franklin Street,
NY 10013
+1 212 431 4646
urbanarchaeology.com

09 Best Made
36 White Street,
NY 10013
+1 646 478 7092
bestmadeco.com

10 Fika
450 Washington Street,
NY 10013
+1 212 706 0565
fikanyc.com

NEIGHBOURHOOD 03
Upper East Side
Rich pickings

In the early 19th century, Manhattan's Upper East Side was little more than green hills sloping from the future site of Central Park to the German immigrant communities of Yorkville near the East River. Bisected by the Boston Post Road, this neighbourhood quickly became a site of suburban homes for families such as the Vanderbilts and Carnegies during the later part of New York's "Gilded Age". Other affluent residents followed suit, building some of the city's grandest limestone-townhouse architecture and giving the area its quaint, old-world character.

The air of affluence still persists, from the stretch of high-fashion retailers and restaurants on Madison Avenue to the culturally rich Museum Mile stretching along 5th Avenue. On the other side of the neighbourhood, the Queensboro Bridge looms large. The 1909 steel beaux arts span was the subject of "The 59th Street Bridge Song (Feelin' Groovy)" by Simon & Garfunkel.

Between these architectural landmarks the art deco Parke-Bernet Building anchors many of the neighbourhood's private art galleries. This was the epicentre of New York's art world in the 1940s and '50s, housing its largest auction house. Today visitors can take in shows at global art powerhouse Gagosian Gallery and conceptual photography at Higher Pictures.

The higher path
Upper East Side walk

Starting off at the 59th Street subway station, zip down to 58th Street and walk towards the East River. At 246 East 58th Street you'll notice a townhouse quite different from its Civil War-era brownstone neighbours. Designed with whitewashed steel latticework in 1989 by Paul Rudolph, **1** *The Modulightor Building* was completed posthumously and is the modernist architect's last building in New York.

Next you need to hang a left on 2nd Avenue and walk north to 61st Street. Turn left here and keep going until you arrive at Madison Avenue. If you've worked up an appetite, dip into **2** *Viand Coffee Shop* for a traditional New York diner breakfast. If you're eager to keep on your feet, order the portable blue-collar New York morning staple: a bacon, egg and cheese sandwich.

Continue northwards up Madison and turn right on 66th until you get to Park Avenue. Here you'll find the **3** *Park Avenue Armory* commanding the entire block. The Armory programmes site-specific performances and installations from artists such as Paul McCarthy and Tom Sachs, who use the building's massive size to realise vast works.

Did you forget that haircut before your New York sojourn? Sit down in one of the four barber chairs at **4** *York Barber Shop* just around the corner on 71st and Lexington Avenue. Small on space but big on charm, this barber has been cutting hair and giving shaves

Central Park

E85th St
E81st St
E78th St
E73rd St
E61st St
E58th St

5th Ave
Madison Ave
Park Ave
Lexington Ave
2nd Ave
1st Ave
2nd Ave
FDR Drive

East River

Getting there

It is very easy to get to this walk thanks to the 4/5/6 trains which run up the entire eastern spine of Central Park on Lexington Avenue. And, hey, some of the stations even have the luxury of digital displays: not always a common sight in New York.

since 1928. When you're fresh-faced and ready for more, head up to 73rd Street and take a left. Just before you hit Central Park, don't miss ⑤*Via Quadronno*. Known for its Milanese sophistication, this espresso bar and panini shop also makes a decadent hot chocolate.

The Upper East Side boasts many of the city's cultural and political consulates. If you walk up to 79th and 5th Avenue you'll discover the ⑥*Albertine* bookshop inside the Cultural Services of the French Embassy. Francophiles

will relish its French and English-language titles, an espresso bar and emerald velvet sofas where you can stare up at the celestial ceiling mural in between chapters.

Walk north along the park and you'll encounter the southernmost edge of the grand Metropolitan Museum of Art – a mightily worthy stop but a day-long affair. Turn onto 81st Street and mid-block you'll discover ⑦*De Vera*, a hushed gallery-sized boutique featuring cabinets stocked with a discerning collection of unique objets d'art, precious curios and antique jewellery. Stroll down 81st Street several blocks and turn left on Lexington Avenue. One block up you'll find the ⑧*Warby Parker* flagship shop housed in a former chemist. The renovated double-storey space features the entire line of its glasses and sunglasses spread between floors via retro-futuristic display tubes.

By now you'll want to rest your feet so walk up to 86th Street and over to 5th Avenue to ⑨*Café Sabarsky*, Neue Galerie's faithful representation of a Viennese coffee house. There you can grab a wine and some goulash before scanning the café's listings for cabaret performances. Don't forget to browse faithful reproductions of Wiener Werkstätte-era home design and personal accessories inside the ⑩*Neue Galerie Design Shop & Book Store* before heading to the 86th Street subway station at Lexington Avenue on your way home. It would also be pretty remiss not to check out the museum, with its collection of early 20th-century Austrian and German art.

Address book

01 The Modulightor Building
   246 East 58th Street,
   NY 10022
02 Viand Coffee Shop
   673 Madison Avenue,
   NY 10065
   +1 212 751 6622
   viandcafeuppereast.com
03 Park Avenue Armory
   643 Park Avenue,
   NY 10065
   +1 212 616 3930
   armoryonpark.org
04 York Barber Shop
   981 Lexington Avenue,
   NY 10021
   +1 212 988 6136
   yorkbarbershop.com
05 Via Quadronno
   25 East 73rd Street,
   NY 10021
   +1 212 650 9880
   viaquadronno.com
06 Albertine
   972 5th Avenue,
   NY 10075
   +1 212 650 0070
   albertine.com
07 De Vera
   26 East 81st Street,
   NY 10028
   +1 212 288 2288
   deveraobjects.com
08 Warby Parker
   1209 Lexington Avenue,
   NY 10028
   +1 646 757 2290
   warbyparker.com
09 Café Sabarsky
   1048 5th Avenue,
   NY 10028
   +1 212 288 0665
   neuegalerie.org
10 Neue Galerie Design
   Shop & Book Store
   1048 5th Avenue,
   NY 10028
   +1 212 628 6200
   neuegalerie.org

NEIGHBOURHOOD 04
Dumbo
New high-flyer

The formerly industrial Brooklyn neighbourhood located underneath the hulking spans of the Brooklyn and Manhattan Bridges was originally called Fulton Landing. Residents in the late 1970s renamed it Dumbo (an acronym that stands for Down Under Manhattan Bridge Overpass), hoping to make it sound unattractive to gentrifying developers. Their tactic didn't work: a late-1990s property boom converted many of the neighbourhood's empty factories and warehouses into offices for burgeoning tech companies and residences for Manhattan transplants now enjoying its unpaved brick streets and East River views.

Dumbo is defined by its waterfront so it's fitting to arrive by sea. The East River Ferry drops visitors at a landing with Brooklyn Bridge Park, an expansive waterfront recreation area that commands superb views of Manhattan. On a sunny afternoon you're sure to see wedding parties and outdoor film screenings on summer nights. This ferry-landing site was originally the location of George Washington's retreat during the Battle of Brooklyn in America's Revolutionary War and is also home to the famed River Café, a diminutive restaurant opened in 1977 when New York City teetered on the edge of bankruptcy and the waterfront was all but devoid of street life.

Bridging the gap
Dumbo walk

If you arrive by the ❶*East River Ferry*, just across the landing on Water Street you'll see what appears to be a lighthouse tower; it is in fact a former fireboat house. Built in 1930, this landmark is today the home of ❷*Brooklyn Ice Cream Factory*, a small-batch ice cream shop offering only classic flavours – from chocolate to butter pecan – all made in-house.

Ice cream cone in hand, take a left on Water Street and walk towards the overpass of the Brooklyn Bridge. This charmingly uneven brick street bends with the waterfront and passes by the Tobacco Warehouse, a pre-Civil War wharf house known for its high archways and star-shaped anchor plates. Take a left on Old Dock Street and walk to the water where you'll find ❸*Jane's Carousel*, a faithfully restored and functional 1922 merry-go-round. In 2011, Pritzker Prize-winning architect Jean Nouvel designed a minimalist glass shed to house the contrasting Baroque amusement, which is fast becoming a Brooklyn landmark.

Once you've dismounted from your carousel horse, walk towards the Manhattan Bridge on Old Plymouth Street and then turn right on Main Street. If you're feeling like a bite or a drink, pop into ❹*Atrium*, a soaring, sun-filled industrial dining room ideal for weekend brunch (try the flank steak with grits) or just a cocktail.

Your nose will most likely lead you to ❺*Almondine Bakery*. There were worrying moments in 2012 after superstorm Sandy flooded the

bakery, causing chef Herve Poussot to halt production – thankfully today he's well and truly back in business. Turn right onto Water Street and head up the stairs of this relaxed French-style spot to grab one of the city's finest almond croissants. Take a right back onto Main Street from Water Street and continue on to Front Street.

Take a left and stroll over to ⑥ *PS Bookshop*, stocked with new and antique books plus museum catalogues with a focus on art and design. Flip through treasures such

as a first edition of Rem Koolhaas's *Delirious New York* or a rare Irving Penn-photographed tome on fashion designer Issey Miyake.

Looking for some music? Duck into long-time New York record shop ⑦ *Halcyon* and browse its collection of eclectic vinyl, from reggae to deep house. To get there, walk down Front Street under the Manhattan Bridge until you hit Pearl Street where you turn left, continuing to Water Street.

Keep going back to Front Street, make a left and you'll be greeted

Getting there

If you're in Chinatown (or Soho for that matter) you could easily reach Dumbo on foot or bicycle via the Manhattan Bridge or take the East River Ferry from Pier 11. Alternatively, the nearest subway stops are York Street on the F train and High Street on the A/C trains.

with the dusty southwestern vibes of ⑧ *Front General Store*, which welcomes visitors with a bookcase of unwieldy cacti and an expansive selection of vintage clothing and Americana artefacts sourced from flea markets around the country. The shop is brimming with museum-like objects including custom-etched Zippo lighters from Vietnam War soldiers and vintage sundries.

It's just three blocks east down Front Street to the postage-stamp-sized enclave of Vinegar Hill, defined more by its townhouses than Dumbo's industrial buildings. End your day with a rustic American dinner at ⑨ *Vinegar Hill House*, located in a low-lit former 19th-century grocery store on the sleepy tree-lined block of Hudson Avenue between Front and Water Streets.

If the sun is setting we encourage you to stroll back to Manhattan across one of the two bridges that terminate in Dumbo. But for the weary walker there is always the York Street subway station just four blocks away.

Address book

01 East River Ferry
Old Fulton Street
and Furman Street,
Brooklyn, NY 11201
+1 800 533 3779
eastriverferry.com

02 Brooklyn Ice Cream
Factory
1 Water Street, NY 11201
+1 718 246 3963
brooklynicecreamfactory.com

03 Jane's Carousel
Dock Street, NY 11201
+1 718 222 2502
janescarousel.com

04 Atrium Dumbo
15 Main Street, NY 11201
+1 718 858 1095
atriumdumbo.com

05 Almondine Bakery
85 Water Street, NY 11201
+1 718 797 5026
almondinebakery.com

06 PS Bookshop
76 Front Street, NY 11201
+1 718 222 3340
psbookshopnyc.com

07 Halcyon
57 Pearl Street, NY 11201
+1 718 260 9299
halcyontheshop.com

08 Front General Store
143 Front Street,
NY 11201
+1 347 693 5328

09 Vinegar Hill House
72 Hudson Avenue,
NY 11201
+1 718 522 1018
vinegarhillhouse.com

NEIGHBOURHOOD 05
West Village
Taste of bohemia

The West Village, a historic home to writers and artists and a cradle for the gay-rights movement, is a welcoming place to get lost. And given that it's one of the few neighbourhoods not to follow New York's legendary grid system, that just might happen. The once bohemian centre is today more of a premium residential quarter that plays host to some of the top retail and restaurant destinations in the city.

Here you can leisurely sate your cultural appetite by simply walking streets that were once home to poets such as Edna St Vincent Millay and the stomping ground of the Beat Generation (think Bob Dylan, Jack Kerouac and Allen Ginsberg). Or you can relive a turning point in modern history by strolling past the Stonewall Inn where the infamous Stonewall riots launched the gay and lesbian liberation movement in 1969.

Today the area is still filled with its fair share of writers and artists but they happen to be less of the struggling variety. The polished air, however, is allied with a neighbourly warmth that can be hard to come by in this busy city. Whether it is a piece of history, a fine retailer or cosy restaurant you're after, the West Village does the trick.

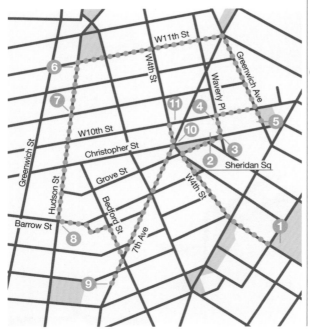

Compelling narrative
West Village walk

① *Washington Square Park* has served as a meeting place since 1827; Mark Twain, Jack Kerouac and Alan Ginsberg all spent time in this space, which in a previous life served as a cemetery. Start here then exit on West 4th Street, passing Cornelia Street to the left. The West Village is filled with quirky landmarks so keep right to notice number 161: Bob Dylan called this home in the 1960s when the rent was $60 per month. Turn right onto Grove Street passing Sheridan Square. **②** *Greenwich Letterpress* will be at Grove's end on Christopher Street; this is worth a stop to satisfy any stationery needs.

On the corner at Waverly Place you'll find **③** *Jeffrey's Grocery*. This

petite bistro is a staple choice for breakfast or lunch, particularly if you can nab a seat by the large windows. Try the escargot toast and a glass of red from Jura or grab a Stumptown coffee and walk along Waverly to **④** *Three Lives & Company*. This independent bookshop is a neighbourhood favourite and the knowledgeable staff always welcome a chat. If you prefer to browse solo, the collection of staff picks is worth a look. After exiting, continue to your right on West 10th Street until it meets Greenwich Avenue where another right turn will bring you to co-ed boutique **⑤** *Personnel*. Here you can find chic items for your wardobe as well as a lovely selection for the home. Walk north up Greenwich Avenue and turn left onto West 11th Street. Continue westward enjoying

Getting there

The quickest route is
via subway stopping at
Christopher Street – Sheridan
Square on the 1 train, or West
4th Street (A/B/C/D/E/F/M
trains) is nearly as good.
If you're using the L line,
you can easily walk from
8th Avenue.

Commerce Street until you reach Bedford Street. Another right turn brings you to the narrowest house in New York, number 75½. Fewer than 3 metres wide, this was once the home of Cary Grant as well as poet Millay. Continue to 7th Avenue where a right turn will take you to underground bar ⑨ *Little Branch*, where top-notch cocktails are often accompanied by live piano and upright bass. This undersized spot is best for appreciating a sophisticated, quiet drink. If you're up for a livelier

time, head back on 7th Avenue towards Christopher Street (the infamous starting point of the gay-rights movement in New York). You will see the storied Stonewall Inn to the right but stop at the nearby corner for a visit to the city's oldest cabaret, ⑩ *The Duplex*. Patrons are normally shoulder-to-shoulder in this piano bar, merrily singing along until closing. Round things off at ⑪ *Smalls Jazz Club* where the last act usually doesn't begin until after midnight.

rows of picturesque brownstones as you head towards Hudson Street, where the traffic becomes busier and you'll find the ⑥ *White Horse Tavern*, a no-frills bar and one of the oldest here. It has hosted a number of the Village's famed literati, including poet Dylan Thomas who spent many evenings here until his resulting death at St Vincent's Hospital a few streets away.

Follow Hudson as far as Charles Street, passing the Monocle Shop. On the right you'll spy Village darling ⑦ *Sweet Corner*. If you're interested in a pastry there isn't a wrong choice at this family operation. There are plenty of places to visit if you're interested in a larger feed so keep heading south down Hudson Street towards the quirky *yakiniku* (Japanese barbecue) restaurant ⑧ *Takashi* on your left just past Barrow Street. If you find yourself craving a midnight snack, save the visit for the wee hours of the morning when Takashi serves its popular ramen.

Afterwards take the winding route on Barrow Street, turning right then continuing along

Address book

01 Washington Square Park
5th Avenue, Waverly Place, West 4th Street and MacDougal Street, NY 10011
nycgovparks.org

02 Greenwich Letterpress
39 Christopher Street, NY 10014
+1 212 989 7464
greenwichletterpress.com

03 Jeffrey's Grocery
172 Waverly Place, NY 10014
+1 646 398 7630
jeffreysgrocery.com

04 Three Lives & Company
154 West 10th Street, NY 10014
+1 212 741 2069
threelives.com

05 Personnel
9 Greenwich Avenue, NY 10014
+1 212 924 0604
personnelofnewyork.com

06 White Horse Tavern
567 Hudson Street, NY 10014
+1 212 989 3956

07 Sweet Corner
535 Hudson Street, NY 10014
+1 212 206 8500
sweetcorner.com

08 Takashi
456 Hudson Street, NY 10014
+1 212 414 2929
takashinyc.com

09 Little Branch
20 7th Avenue South, NY 10011
+1 212 929 4360

10 The Duplex
61 Christopher Street, NY 10014
+1 212 255 5438
theduplex.com

11 Smalls Jazz Club
183 West 10th Street, NY 10014
+1 646 476 4346
smallsjazzclub.com

Resources
— Inside knowledge

OK, so the subway is a little grimy but it's also an incredible means of crossing town: a vast network stretching into the outer boroughs and a 24-hour service even during the holidays. So grab a MetroCard and get on board (although using the bus, a bike or your own feet are also decent options, as you'll see). The subway can be confusing (*see our essay on page 74*) but we've got some succinct advice and there aren't too many other pitfalls you need to ready yourself for.

With your earphones locked to the countless songs that have been inspired by NYC (we've proffered some favourites) you're ready to eat, drink, sleep, work and digest some culture. If you're a British English speaker you may occasionally feel like you're speaking a completely different language to New Yorkers so we've also tried to give you a heads-up on that front.

Transport
Get around town

01 Subway: A weekly subway card ($31) means you can avoid the kiosks, or you can grab a single-ride ticket ($2.75). Clock the exact speed at which you should swipe said passes; it's all in the wrist and will mean less faffing at the turnstile.
mta.info

02 Bicycle: With Citibike you can ride with ease just about anywhere in Manhattan; a nice way to stay above ground and take advantage of a growing number of routes. One-day hire costs $9.95; seven days are yours for $25.
citibikenyc.com

03 Ferry: Taking to New York's waterways can be a welcome reprieve from other modes of transport and you can't beat the views of Lower Manhattan. A single ride is $9; an all-day pass is $31.
nywatertaxi.com

04 Bus: Really the only way to cross town on public transport if Central Park is in your way. Use your MetroCard or have exact change for a $2.75 single journey.
mta.info

05 On foot: The wide avenues that divide Manhattan from north to south can be intimidating if you're not used to crossing them. Worry not: there will be a throng of New Yorkers waiting for the light to turn. Follow them and remember to look right.

06 Taxi and private car hire: Compared to other cities, the meters in a yellow cab don't run nearly as high. Or if you prefer a private vehicle book with Strictly Confidential Service or Ozo Car.
strictlyconfidentialservice.com; ozocar.com

07 Flights: If you're not flying commercial, Teterboro is the private airport of choice, 19km from midtown Manhattan.
panynj.gov

Vocabulary
Local lingo

Beyond remembering the below, we'd recommend trying to wrap your head around New York's many neighbourhood acronyms, which you can find in the Need to Know section (*see page 14*).

01 B&T: commuters from outside Manhattan
02 Bodega: corner shop
03 Buck: dollar
04 Check: bill
05 Dime: 10¢ coin
06 Entrée: main course
07 Nickel: 5¢ coin
08 Schmear: bagel spread
09 The Village: West Village
10 Walk-up: building without lift

Soundtrack to the city
Five top tunes

Turn up the speakers for our genre-spanning New York playlist.

01 Miles Davis, 'Kind of Blue': Never was New York's pathos and beauty better captured than in 1959 at Columbia Records on 30th Street, when this perfect album was improvised into being.
02 Simon & Garfunkel, 'The Only Living Boy in New York': It's the late 1960s, Art Garfunkel left to shoot a film and Paul Simon sang away the loneliness of New York.
03 Odyssey, 'Native New Yorker': Never before and never again would disco music and New York reach these heights of groovy sentimentality.
04 Stevie Wonder, 'Living for the City': The life of a New Yorker only just getting by, told to strict rhythms with irrepressible funk.
05 Beastie Boys, 'No Sleep till Brooklyn': It was meant to be the Beastie Boys' snub at heavy metal but this song became the anthem of a borough and its late-night adventurism.

Best events
What to see

01 Armory Arts Week, various venues: Contemporary and modern-art fair with events held throughout the week.
March, thearmoryshow.com

02 Tribeca Film Festival, various venues: New York's premier fest for independent, documentary and short films.
April, tribecafilm.com

03 NYCxDesign, various venues: Visit contemporary-furniture fairs at ICFF and the best of 20th-century at the Collective Design Fair.
May, nycxdesign.com

04 Frieze New York: Outpost of the London-based art fair that has been bringing top international art galleries together on Randall's Island since 2012.
May, friezenewyork.com

05 Northside, Brooklyn: Williamsburg and Greenpoint play host to hundreds of musicians.
June, northsidefestival.com

06 Renegade Craft Fair, various venues: A top selection of independent homeware and jewellery.
June, September and November, renegadecraft.com

07 Hudson River Park summer events, various venues: Head riverside for everything from salsa dancing to an outdoor cinema.
July to August, hudsonriverpark.org

08 Lincoln Center Music Festival: A stacked line-up of theatre, opera, dance, music, puppetry and more.
July to August, lincolncenterfestival.org

09 US Open, Queens: This is the place to check out a handsome crowd – and the tennis isn't bad either.
August to September, usopen.org

10 New York City Marathon, citywide: If you're not racing, watch events unfold in any of the five boroughs.
November, tcsnycmarathon.org

Rainy day
Weather-proof activities

In a temperate climate like New York's it's tough to predict exactly when there will be rainfall. Luckily, when it does strike, there is a surplus of cultural venues and plenty of welcoming bars.

01 The Metropolitan Museum of Art: New York is hardly lacking when it comes to cultural institutions but the Met, bordering Central Park, is the don. You could happily get lost here for a day – actually, more like a week – and still only cover a small amount of ground; this place is gargantuan. If it's foul outside you could check out some of the 26,000 Egyptian artefacts. And if the sun does happen to come out? Head straight for the rooftop bar.
metmuseum.org

02 New York Public Library: You don't need a library card to take refuge in this beautiful building on 5th Avenue and 42nd Street should the weather run amok. There are millions of books to peruse and surely one of the world's most grandiose reading rooms in the world (wooden tables, ceiling frescoes and chandeliers) to read your selection in.
nypl.org

03 Cosy bars: New York may be the city of rooftop drinking establishments but it also knows how to protect you from inclement weather. From light-filled conservatories to chase away the drabness (Café Mogador and The Ludlow) to a winter-time chalet room (Café Select), NY has, quite literally, got it covered.
Café Mogador, Williamsburg cafemogador.com
The Ludlow, Lower East Side ludlowhotel.com
Café Select, Nolita cafeselectnyc.com

(For more bar ideas see Food and drink from page 28)

Sunny day
The great outdoors

New Yorkers flood outdoors in sunny weather, whether it's to dine alfresco, stroll through a farmers' market or surf at Rockaway Beach. Here are a few ideas for the best places to take in this vibrant city.

01 Rockaways: Though a bit of a trek from Manhattan, a visit to the Rockaways is an afternoon well spent on a warm, sunny day – and the Queens-set beaches are accessible by subway. It was entirely revamped post-Hurricane Sandy and you can grab a pint and an arepa (flatbread) at the 86th, 97th or 106th Street beaches on the modern boardwalk. Or, if you're feeling more adventurous, take your first surf lesson.

02 Brooklyn Flea: Brooklyn Flea has several locations but Fort Greene's 3,700 sq m schoolyard at Bishop Loughlin Memorial High School is our preference. Like a bustling town square, this market is packed on Saturdays from April to November with vintage knick-knacks and the best of Brooklyn's street food. Come prepared to spend a few hours: the place is chock-full of goodies.
brooklynflea.com

03 Public Art Fund: The Public Art Fund has been installing art on the streets of New York since 1977. As a result, culture is at your fingertips on a sunny day without ever having to venture indoors. Of the Fund's hundreds of installations, past projects include works such as Olaf Breuning's painted aluminium "Clouds" in Central Park and Jeff Koons' oversized topiary-like sculpture "Split-Rocker" at Rockefeller Center. For a schedule and locations of the artworks, visit the website.
publicartfund.org

About Monocle
—— Step inside

In 2007, Monocle was launched as a monthly magazine briefing on global affairs, business, culture, design and much more. We believed there was a globally minded audience of readers who were hungry for opportunities and experiences beyond their national borders.

Today Monocle is a complete media brand with print, audio and online elements – not to mention our expanding network of shops and cafés. Besides our London HQ we have seven international bureaux in New York, Toronto, Istanbul, Singapore, Tokyo, Zürich and Hong Kong. We continue to grow and flourish and at our core is the simple belief that there will always be a place for a print brand that is committed to telling fresh stories and sending photographers on assignments. It's also a case of knowing that our success is all down to the readers, advertisers and collaborators who have supported us along the way.

❶ International bureaux
Capital connections

MONOCLE's Noho bureau is an integral part of the brand, co-ordinating and commissioning our network of writers and correspondents in the Americas and producing stories from our New York hub, across the country and travelling into the Spanish-speaking world south of the border. Our bureau is headed up by Ed Stocker, with support from deputy bureau chief Megan Billings. The team are also regulars on Monocle 24 and ensure a steady stream of guests appear on our live shows, via the bureau studio, to discuss everything from politics and business to design, literature and art.

❷ Radio
Sound approach

Monocle 24 is our round-the-clock radio station that was launched in 2011. It delivers global news and shows covering foreign affairs, urbanism, business, culture, food and drink, design and print media. When you find yourself in the US you can listen to *The Globalist*, our morning news programme; Monocle 24's editors, presenters and guests set the agenda in international news and business. We also have a playlist to accompany you day and night, regularly assisted by live sessions that are hosted at our Midori House headquarters.

❸ Online
Digital delivery

We also have a dynamic website: *monocle.com*. As well as being the place to hear Monocle 24, we use the site to present our films, which are beautifully shot and edited by our in-house team and provide a fresh perspective on our stories. Check out the films celebrating the cities that make up our Travel Guide Series before you explore the rest of the site.